COLORADO
MYTHS & LEGENDS

THE TRUE STORIES BEHIND HISTORY'S MYSTERIES

SECOND EDITION

JAN ELIZABETH MURPHY

TWODOT®

GUILFORD, CONNECTICUT
HELENA, MONTANA

A · TWODOT® · BOOK

TwoDot is an imprint of Globe Pequot.
TwoDot is a registered trademark of Rowman & Littlefield.

Distributed by NATIONAL BOOK NETWORK

British Library Cataloguing in Publication Information Available

Library of Congress Cataloging-in-Publication Data

ISBN 978-1-4930-2318-9
ISBN 978-1-4930-2319-6 (ebook)

∞™ The paper used in this publication meets the minimum requirements of American National Standard for Information Sciences—Permanence of Paper for Printed Library Materials, ANSI/NISO Z39.48-1992.

To
Jani McCarty

For helping me to
remember who I am
and empowering me
to thrive.

CONTENTS

COLORADO

NEBRASKA

KANSAS

OKLAHOMA

NEW MEXICO

UTAH

WYOMING

GREAT PLAINS

FRONT RANGE

ROCKY MOUNTAINS

100 MILES

100 KILOMETERS

South Platte River

Arkansas River

Big Sandy Creek

Purgatoire River

DENVER

BUFFALO BILL'S GRAVE

BARNUM

GOLDEN

RED ROCKS

IDLEDALE

MOTHER CABRINI SHRINE

GEORGETOWN

FAIRPLAY

GRANBY

LEADVILLE

PUEBLO

Arkansas River

GREAT SAND DUNES NATIONAL PARK

ALAMOSA

Rio Grande

GLENWOOD SPRINGS

Colorado River

MEEKER

Yampa River

White River

DURANGO

HOVENWEEP NATIONAL MONUMENT

MESA VERDE NATIONAL PARK

Dolores River

San Juan River

ACKNOWLEDGMENTS

Thank you to the following:

The Jefferson County Public Library, Lakewood, Colorado— always very helpful.

Mother Cabrini Shrine, Golden, Colorado.

History Colorado, the Colorado Historical Society.

Western History Collection, Denver Public Library.

Stephanie Hester, my first book editor, for making it such a joy.

Courtney Oppel, for being my editor twice, and continuing the joy.

And for my dear cousin and friend, Ann Wilson, who saw me through the most difficult times.

For my other dear friends, for their constant love, support, and encouragement:

Darilyn Woodaman	Andrea Vining Huggins
Kathy Zornes Samsel	Diane Fuchs
Jan Pond	Pat Jurgens

ACKNOWLEDGMENTS

Maro Lorimer

Glenna Bissegger

Marilyn Parris Garcia

Jan Wheeler Hadley

Hilarie Anderson Byrnes

Julie Armour

Laura Figuli

Sheralyn Austin-Gagne

Barb DeCaro

Maryanne Bach Andrle

Arlene Fitterer

Catherine Scott

Dawn Browne

Janet Redford

Jill Long

Sara C. E. Lang

Ann Bolson

Anita Martin

INTRODUCTION

Colorado is full of myths and legends. With some of the highest peaks on the continent, deepest canyons, one-of-a-kind geological features, and broadest open prairies, the stage has been set for a fascinating array of dramas. Strange, sometimes unbelievable occurrences have unfolded across the state.

The tallest sand dunes on the North American continent are located in Colorado. Some of them reach as high as 700 feet from base to summit. But why are these uncommon formations here, in the middle of the Rocky Mountains?

The abandonment, by those ancient Native Americans called the Anasazi, of their cliff homes in southwestern Colorado will always make us wonder what happened there. The distinctive arid canyons, containing the deeply set alcoves and caves where their dwellings were ensconced, are part of the mystery. Why did these people leave the area forever? And why did they build and then abandon hundreds of towers in the area of Hovenweep?

The geology of Colorado lured gold and silver miners in the 1800s. The Reynolds Gang, fortune hunter Baby Doe Tabor, and wanderer Louis Dupuy all had hopes of securing their financial futures in mining. But where did the Reynoldses bury their treasure? Why did the "rags to riches to rags" Baby Doe Tabor die in poverty when she didn't have to? And what secret was Louis Dupuy hiding?

Wide-open spaces and unexplored lands beckoned legendary figures such as Mother Cabrini, P. T. Barnum, and Buffalo Bill. How did Mother Cabrini perform her miracle in the foothills? What Colorado events surrounded the life of the great circus man, P. T. Barnum? Was Buffalo Bill buried on Lookout Mountain by choice?

Further mysteries make one ask: Why do people think that aliens visited a ranch in southern Colorado? And did a professor at the University of Colorado disappear because he was a spy? Bridey Murphy made national headlines when, under hypnosis, she revealed facts about having lived a past life in Ireland, although she had never been there in her present life. Is this possible? How do you explain the "Granby Idol," a 1,000-year-old stone artifact unearthed on the Western Slope?

And even a street in Denver holds its own secret that will always remain a mystery. It was named Colfax for an obscure and uninspiring US Speaker of the House. Why?

Ute Chief Colorow and Antoinette Perry became legends in their own time, yet their lives were mostly unknown. How could this happen? Read on!

CHAPTER ONE
THE GREAT SAND DUNES

Rising 700 feet in the air and stretching for 10 miles, the Great Sand Dunes of Colorado are one of the most striking and mysterious geological features in America. For many who visit there, little thought is given to how these dunes got there. It is just considered one giant sandbox!

On any nice spring day in late May, and especially on the Memorial Day weekend, a crowd of visitors fills the campgrounds and parking lots around the Great Sand Dunes National Park near Alamosa, Colorado. Most are in swimsuits or shorts, and some are carrying beach balls, large beach umbrellas, chaise lounges, and beach towels. Some have colorful kid-sized plastic shovels and buckets. But where's the beach?

Just ahead, sand dunes reach into the sky. Behind the tall dunes, mountain peaks rise up to 10,000 feet, with snow still clinging to the highest points. It certainly doesn't look like a desert. But if you look back down to the sand dunes, visions of camels with robed Arabs on their backs do not seem out of place.

Then there's an even odder scene. Gushing out of the mountains, Medano Creek winds around the flat base of the dunes and runs across the sand. It's a small creek , granted, and when it spreads

As visitors to Colorado's Great Sand Dunes know, there are few sights so startling as coming upon dunes in the middle of the mountains.

out over the sand, much of it gets soaked up, but small rivulets manage to survive the crossing. An odd characteristic of this water flowing across the sand is that it changes course back and forth across the wide expanse.

Visitors pitch their umbrellas in the sand along the bank. The water never gets deeper than a few inches, and while it's seldom more than several yards across, the area of wet sand can be more than 50 feet wide. It's like one big beach, but with a very "low tide" and no ocean.

Memorial Day weekend is so popular at the Great Sand Dunes because this small creek comes only from spring snowmelt. Most of the year, the sandy "beach scene" is dry. And if there has been a particularly dry year with little snow in the higher mountains, the precious "beach days" when the water runs across the sands may be short in number.

Why does the water shift and change directions as it moves over the sand? The rivulets displace patterns of sand, digging down and creating small dams that then block the water flow and redirect it. The process is repeated time and time again. And while the water is moving along the bases of the dunes, the wind is blowing over the tops, constantly changing their shapes.

And how did the dunes form originally? Most believe that the secret lies in the flat and semiarid plain of the San Luis Valley. Grains of sand are picked up by the wind from the valley and carried toward the high peaks to the east. But because the sand is too heavy for the wind to lift it over the mountains, it falls to the earth again and creates the dunes.

So why don't the sand dunes push right up against the higher mountains to the east? Medano Creek, which runs along the base of the mountains, carries this sand back out to the valley, so the dunes don't have a chance to take hold next to the mountains.

Long before geologists came up with these scientific answers, there existed a number of legends and myths. One story from 1885 tells of a herd of sheep that was covered in sand, providing the seeds for the first dune. In this fable some sheepherders came to the San Luis Valley in 1816, bringing 3,500 sheep along with them. They were to locate in a pasture where there was good grazing. These men built small houses and corrals to care for the sheep. One day, a sheepherder went to explore the surrounding mountains and was gone for three days. When he returned, he could not find the original camp. There was now a huge amount of sand, 50 feet deep, that had buried the whole area. He went for help, but when they returned to dig for the men, the sand was too deep and would fall back into the holes as they dug. They realized that all of the men, the houses, corrals, and the 3,500 sheep had been buried by a storm under the huge mound of sand. None of them was ever found. Each year thereafter the storms blew in more sand until eventually the Great Sand Dunes were formed.

Another fable from the Ute Indians tells how the sand dunes saved a young girl's life after she had first been captured and then later sold to a rancher by a Ute chief. The rancher borrowed money from his rich brother to free the little girl and raise her in his own home. Later, however, the chief decided he wanted the girl back. When the rancher refused, the Ute fought with him. The two men fatally wounded each other and died among the dunes. When a storm came up, they were buried under mounds of blowing sand and could not be found. Many years later, a storm shifted the dunes again, and human bones were uncovered. Some believed that this was where the two men had died and that their sand-covered bodies had formed the first mounds of the Great Sand Dunes.

Although these legends are no doubt more fiction than fact, the blowing sand has indeed been known to bury whatever is in its path. Even today, a visitor to the Great Sand Dunes National Park can locate part of a forest along its edge that is gradually being buried alive. The skeletons of old dead trees can be seen sticking out of the sand.

Another mystery about the Great Sand Dunes is how they have continued to grow in size and yet remain relatively stable.

Before modern geology solved the riddle, there were many mysteries and legends about how the dunes might have originated.

Many think that the local streams and snowstorms have deposited enough water to keep the underlying sand wet. This keeps the sand dunes in place while the drier sand on top continues to blow and drift.

One final mystery takes place near the Great Sand Dunes. It is an underground waterfall and, until recently, only a few early explorers had known of its existence. Even today, though, the average visitor to the national park is unaware of it. The waterfall is found deep in a cave and, when frozen, is said to be a brilliant aqua blue. It is unknown where this water comes from or why it has such brilliant color when it's frozen.

What is not a mystery any longer is how to visit these falls. They can be reached by taking the gravel road located on the

Bureau of Land Management property 4 miles east of Colorado Highway 150, just south of the entrance to the Great Sand Dunes National Park. In winter the approach can be made by walking in along the ice floor of the cavern.

Even with all the mysteries and legends that have become part of the lore about the Great Sand Dunes, most people have come to regard the dunes as simply a fun place to visit. The park service allows and encourages tourists to walk, run, and roll down the dunes. This is most comfortably experienced during the cooler months when the sand is not so warm that it burns a hiker's bare feet. And the park offers other features such as hiking along Medano Creek or up the trails to the mountaintops nearby. But on a hot summer day, the temperature of the sand can reach 140 degrees Fahrenheit. No mystery about that!

CHAPTER TWO
THE ANASAZI

A l Wetherill stood on the canyon floor and stared at the archaeological ruins above him. "Who were the people who had lived here?" he wondered. "Where had they come from? And where did they go?"

In 1882 Benjamin Alfred Wetherill, a rancher who lived on the nearby Alamo Ranch with his brothers, was visiting Mancos Cañon in southwestern Colorado. He'd had a tip from a stranger who had recently wintered his stock there. Al had always been curious about native artifacts and had found many mounds, pottery shards, and artifacts on his family's land, but this was obviously something quite different.

He rode his horse down Mancos Cañon about 12 miles, initially seeing nothing out of the ordinary. With dusk approaching, he decided to go back. As he turned his pony around on the trail, however, his attention was caught by the rim of a cave about 100 feet directly above him. He dismounted and scrambled up the rocky slope. There it was, just as the man had said. Obviously man-made rock walls painted with white stripes stood silent and uninhabited. Pottery fragments and flint chips were scattered throughout the dwelling. Later discoveries at this location would also reveal large

With 150 rooms, the Cliff Palace ruin in Mesa Verde National Park is the largest prehistoric cliff structure in North America.

numbers of sandals in the debris, giving the dwelling its name, Sandal House. It would be among dozens of canyon cliff dwellings that would eventually be discovered by the Wetherills during the next several years.

This discovery led to the eventual establishment of what is now called Mesa Verde National Park. It is the only national park that features human culture as its main point of interest. And it is the only place where Native Americans left more than petroglyphs on rock walls or arrowheads and bone tools. Here are the rock houses where they had lived, built right into the cliffs. As more and more of these cliff dwellings came to be discovered throughout the canyons of the mesa, it was evident that this entire area had contained a huge settlement of ancient people. Some buildings were two or three stories high, and all had been built with such precision and craft that they were still standing when Al Wetherill discovered them more than 500 years later. It could be described as a Native American ghost town.

Having no name to call these early cliff dwellers, modern archaeologists refer to them as the Anasazi—a Navajo word meaning "the ancient ones." And sometimes they are referred to as the ancient Puebloans.

So who were these people? Why did they build rock houses up in the cliffs? And why did they desert their homes after living there for so many years?

Al Wetherill's findings at Sandal House and other dwellings were the earliest actual archaeological collections from the area, but nearby native tribes were already very familiar with these dwellings. They spoke of them as being "forbidden," however, and tended to avoid them. No reason has ever been given for the Indians' fear of these locations. Once the cliff dwellings were abandoned, no natives ever returned to live there again.

The first actual recorded sighting of the cliff dwellings happened in 1776 when a Catholic priest, Father Silvestre Vélez de Escalante, traveled from Santa Fe, New Mexico, to explore the area. Between 1846 and 1848 a US military expedition, conducted by Major John Wesley Powell, and a separate US Geological Survey both documented seeing "ruined buildings of an ancient race" as they passed Mesa Verde. But the cliff dwellings remained mostly unknown to the outside world until Wetherill started exploring deep into the canyons, documenting and collecting artifacts in the area.

Unfortunately, potential answers to the mystery of what became of the Anasazi cliff dwellers may have been lost forever in the years after Al Wetherill made his discovery in 1882 and before the Mesa Verde National Park was established in 1906. After word of Wetherill's findings became common knowledge, souvenir hunters descended, picking through the ruins to remove unknown numbers of artifacts.

One of the many early travelers who visited the cliff dwellings was photographer William Henry Jackson. Jackson's photographs reveal Mesa Verde as it was more than one hundred years ago. This photo record provides some idea of just how much has been lost. Technically the artifacts were not "stolen" since there was no official law protecting them until the park was established. Many items were removed just for the purpose of selling them back to the archaeological community. Although some of the items were saved, much of the understanding about these artifacts was lost because they were removed from their original locations and, as a result, could never be studied in their historical context.

Wetherill and his brothers were both a part of the problem and a part of the solution. Although they removed hundreds of artifacts from the original locations, they also took a sincere interest in documenting what they found. And they finally gave much of their collection to the archaeologists. Most of it is now housed at the museum in the national park. The Wetherill brothers also provided invaluable information in locating the many cliff dwellings in the vast network of canyons in the mesa (although even the Wetherills did not find them all).

Despite the missing pieces there is enough evidence remaining to lead scientific authorities to some possible conclusions. Lifestyle, weather, and location all may have played a part in the final disappearance of the Anasazi. Studies suggest that the Mesa Verde area was first settled as early as ad 1. By the late 1200s the general abandonment of the area had begun, and by the year 1300, the Anasazi had disappeared from the region altogether.

The earliest Native Americans in the Southwest were nomadic, surviving by hunting and gathering. They used spears to kill buffalo, deer, and other animals, and plant food came from whatever was growing wild. A common practice was to follow buffalo herds so they could stay close to their food supply. Between 2000 and 1500 bc they had begun to establish farms.

Using primarily sandstone, mortar, and wooden beams, the ancestral Puebloans managed to build some of America's most intriguing structures.

DENVER PUBLIC LIBRARY, WESTERN HISTORY COLLECTION, HARRY M. RHOADS, RH-274

By about 1000 bc, they were weaving baskets for storing water and food. And by 500 bc their farms began to include corn and, later, squash. Farming allowed the tribes to settle in one place, although they still were nomadic in nongrowing seasons. The natives became highly skilled at basket weaving and began to incorporate designs.

Around ad 550 the people who would become known as the Anasazi moved from the valley floors to the tops of the mesas, where it was cooler in summer and warmer in winter. There was also more rain and better soil for growing their crops. Plentiful trees provided wood for tools, buildings, and fuel for fires. In these early years on the mesa, they lived in pit houses below ground. They began making clay pots, which replaced the baskets, and they also began using clay for adobe houses built above ground. By ad 750 the Pueblo Era had begun, and they were building their houses out of stone. Their pottery became more and more advanced and was decorated with ornate designs.

It was not until about ad 1200 that the Anasazi made the radical move to the cliff caves, leaving the mesa top. Why did such a drastic change in their lifestyle occur? Some believe the Anasazi were experiencing a large growth in population and that the mesa top was becoming crowded. Or perhaps more land for farming was needed, and by moving into the cliffs, they were making more farmland available. They may also have discovered that the cliff caves provided excellent protection from the wind, rain, and snow. Others suggest that they may have been threatened by some outside enemy tribe and the cliff dwellings provided safety from attack as well as a view of approaching enemies.

But this move was to be short lived for the Anasazi. They lived there fewer than a hundred years. By the late 1200s evidence shows that the Anasazi had deserted the cliff dwellings and left the area forever.

Why did they leave? Some evidence suggests that it may have had to do with the changing weather. One of their most important food sources was corn (corncob remains have been found throughout the cliff dwellings). Prior to the mid-1200s rainfall had been plentiful enough to grow it and other crops. But scientists have determined that a drought began around the year 1276. Year after year following this date, there was little snow or rain. Farming would have become almost impossible. Crop yields would have seriously diminished. This would have made the area uninhabitable.

It's likely that their numbers simply grew beyond the limits of their resources, as defined by the drought. Evidence supports the fact that their population was increasing steadily throughout this time period, since larger and larger cliff dwellings were being built.

Additionally, crops may have been further hobbled by plant diseases. Blight and insect problems often increase with drought conditions. Supplies of trees for building and for fuel may have become exhausted. Although most buildings were made of stone, wood was used in the construction of the ceilings and other supports. They also needed trees for their firewood. Even apart from the drought, a shortage of trees could have ended their normal way of life.

There is also some evidence that the Anasazi may have been threatened by an outside enemy. Some skeletal remains have been found with fractures or holes in the skulls. Could they have been attacked by enemies? Other tribes may have desired their success-ful location on the cooler mesa. Or their success could have evoked envy from the poorer tribes in the region. But if there was an enemy, they did not move into Mesa Verde when the Anasazi left. This too would suggest that the area was no longer habitable.

Still another theory suggests that other tribes to the south who traded with the Anasazi believed in human sacrifice. Could the Anasazi have been influenced or even dominated by another tribe's self-destructive belief system?

Most experts believe that the gradual disintegration of natural conditions is the most likely reason for the demise of the Anasazi society. It has even been suggested that the Anasazi could merely have opted for the more benevolent physical conditions to the south. Modern studies suggest that it is most likely that the Ana-sazi went south and merged with the Pueblo peoples. These tribes include the Hopi, Laguna, Zuni, and Acoma. About ad 1300 the numbers of the Pueblo populations near what is now Santa Fe, New Mexico, and along the Rio Grande River, began to increase at a high rate.

Some stories told by Pueblo people say that their ancestors once lived in the canyons of Mesa Verde. They are likely right. But why these ancient people moved away from their ancestral home will probably always remain a mystery.

CHAPTER THREE
THE REYNOLDS TREASURE

There's something about the idea of hunting for buried treasure that is always thrilling to contemplate. And when that concept is placed in the Old West and it involves money and jewels stolen by Colorado outlaws, well, it's hard to resist a little speculation.

Since 1864, when the Reynolds outlaw gang ran wild through Colorado, there has been relentless speculation regarding what happened to the loot they stole. None of it was ever recovered from the gang members who were arrested or killed. And what of the members who escaped? There's no evidence that they took it with them. There are those who still believe that the treasure lies buried out there somewhere.

It all began when a young man named Jim Reynolds came to Fairplay, Colorado, in 1863. He'd been born and raised in Texas in the early 1840s and had decided it was time to strike out on his own.

Fairplay sits surrounded by mountains in the middle of a sprawling and beautiful valley called South Park. The area was mostly empty until the West's "second" gold rush in 1859 (the first big gold rush having occurred ten years earlier in 1849 in California). As the California mines began to play out, miners drifted back to Colorado even as new prospectors were coming from the East. These new immigrants were called "the 59ers." A gold strike in the mountains near Denver had set off this new influx of fortune seekers.

When Jim Reynolds arrived in Fairplay, the town was a burgeoning community of miners living in tents, ramshackle huts, and log houses on muddy streets. The miners were there to find gold and silver ore, and all were looking to strike it rich. Reynolds had met up with a few buddies along the way, and together they tried to find their fortunes in the mines. They couldn't hold down a job, however, perhaps either because manual labor did not suit them or because their drinking and brawling at night made them unfit to work the next morning. But even after giving up work entirely, they still seemed to have plenty of money to spend. This did not go unnoticed in the community. Several thefts of nominal amounts of money had occurred, and Reynolds and his cronies were suspected. Stagecoaches were also being held up. And even though stage stations typically kept only small amounts of money on hand, the robbers were stealing from them too.

Eventually, a larger robbery was attempted. The Spotswood and McClelland stagecoach was held up, but this time a posse was waiting, and the thieves were caught in the act. Most of the hoodlums successfully escaped, but Jim Reynolds was arrested and taken to jail in Denver.

Jailhouses of that era were log shacks at best, and it wasn't long before Jim and a couple of his cellmates managed to escape. Reynolds went back to Texas, and although this was the height of the Civil War, he decided not to join the Confederacy as a soldier.

Instead, he organized his own guerrilla unit. His plan was to steal Colorado gold and silver and then bring it back to the South to help fund the war.

He found twenty-three men to join him, including his younger brother, John Reynolds. In the spring of 1864, Jim Reynolds led his group out of Texas toward Colorado Territory. Although he said he had been commissioned by the Texas Confederate Forces, a record of this appointment has never been found. He was apparently devoted to his cause, though, because all of his guerrilla volunteers were required to take an oath of allegiance.

While passing through New Mexico Territory on their way to Colorado Territory, the group happened upon a wagon train. It was too tempting a target to pass up. They robbed it of $60,000.

The gang disappeared into the Spanish Peaks, biding their time until the search had been abandoned. The men, with nothing on their minds except the thought of all that money, began to instigate an uprising against Reynolds. He maintained that the minted coins they had stolen were to be used for the Confederacy. Conveniently forgetting their oaths, most of the men wanted their share of the loot then and there.

Reynolds had no choice but to pay them, although he demanded that they leave his gang. Most of his guerrillas were happy to comply. When the remainder of the gang traveled on to Colorado Territory, they numbered only nine members, including Jim and his brother, John, Owen Singleterry, Jake Stowe, Tom Holliman, John Babbitt, John Andrews, Jack Robinson, and Tom Knight. They briefly scattered to avoid drawing attention and then reconvened at a ranch between Hartsel and Fairplay. Jim Reynolds knew ranch

COLORADO MYTHS & LEGENDS

owner Adolph Guirand and his wife from his earlier days in Colorado Territory. The Guirands may not have expected or desired their new guests, but the gang was fed and sheltered there.

Moving on toward Fairplay, the gang began to pillage on behalf of the South. The first encounters were relatively minor. They came across the superintendent of the Phillips Lode mine, Major H. H. deMary, and emptied his pockets. DeMary was rumored to keep gold in buckets and jars. Unfortunately, he was only carrying a few dollars. Reynolds decided to take him with them as a prisoner.

As they headed toward McLaughlin's stage station, a few more robberies along the way also yielded little. But Reynolds had been tipped off that the McLaughlin stage was carrying a rich shipment, and that became his main target.

At McLaughlin's, 10 miles outside of Fairplay, the gang rode in and took over the station. After disarming the occupants, Reynolds ordered the cook to fix them dinner. The gang wined and dined, apparently enjoying themselves immensely.

When the stage arrived, the only passenger was the owner of the line. He was robbed of about $400 and a gold watch. The driver was ordered to hand over the mail, and the strongbox was forced open with an ax. It would later be rumored that the gang stole anywhere from $3,000 to $100,000 in currency, gold, and jewelry. The guerrillas also stole the horses and, before riding off, chopped the spokes out of the wheels of the stage. Then they freed Major deMary.

Mail was of utmost importance to people on the frontier. Not only was it the only way to stay in contact with friends and relatives, but for some it was a way to transfer money back home. A Fairplay prostitute had mailed $200 to her sick mother in Springfield, Illinois. When she heard the stage had been robbed, she was bereft and angry. Others had also lost important documents and funds.

Although the alert had gone out to many local communities after this robbery, the Reynolds gang proceeded with little haste. As they moved northeast toward a way station called Michigan House, they stole more horses. When they reached Kenosha Pass, they stopped for a meal at the Kenosha House. (The use of "house" in the name is derived from the then popular term of "road house," a resting place for travelers). The gang then pressed on eastward to Omaha House, where they decided to stop and relax for a while.

A lone man from the town of Hamilton, Mr. Berry, had been tracking the gang ever since the incident at the McLaughlin stage station. At Kenosha Pass he found a man named Mr. Hall to accompany him. They arrived at Omaha House but were promptly captured by Reynolds. Berry and Hall's pistols were taken from them, as well as Hall's necktie pin.

The gang was in good spirits and talked easily with Berry and Hall. They told them they had come to Colorado Territory to steal gold, silver, and treasure for the Confederacy. One of the gang pulled pieces of stolen stage mail from his pocket and joked about it. Finally they released the two men, even returning Hall's pin to him after learning that it had been given to him by a friend. Berry and Hall left Omaha House and rode to the nearby Junction House, at the intersection of roads to Evergreen and Denver. They warned the local residents about the gang and then continued on to Denver.

Reynolds and his gang, hiding outside of Junction House, were still unaware of any potential trouble. Even though the residents had been warned, the gang was able to quietly steal more horses without being seen. They returned to Omaha House for another night.

They did not know that several different posses were headed their way. Captain Maynard's group had set out from Denver, as had Marshal Dave Cook and his group. Jack Sparks from Swan River (near Breckenridge) was leading a posse down from the north. And Major deMary, who had earlier been robbed by the gang, had formed a posse of thirty men and was coming from Fairplay.

Reynolds was very familiar with this territory, and the next day he chose to lead his gang up to Shaffer's Crossing. He saw deMary's posse down below, heading in his direction, and for the first time he became aware that it was no longer safe to travel out

Bandit Jim Reynolds came to Fairplay, Colorado, in 1863.

in the open. He decided to lead his band off the main road onto a mountain trail up Handcart Gulch. Here they built a makeshift camp and a corral for their horses. A lookout was posted to watch the valley below.

While they waited, they might have had an opportunity to bury their treasure. The gold, silver, and cash would have probably been cumbersome, but they would have had no real need to unload it until they knew they were being pursued. If they had wanted to stash it in order to move faster, this would have been a likely place.

Major deMary's posse continued along the main road, passing by the trail down which Reynolds had led his gang. Captain Maynard's posse arrived at Kenosha House only to find that the gang had already left. They headed back to Denver. Cook's group continued on to Fairplay, missing everyone.

Without knowing it, Jack Sparks's posse was headed directly toward the gang's camp. Sparks and his men had arrived at the top of Handcart Gulch at nightfall and decided to camp there. One of Sparks's men thought he saw a flicker of light through the woods. On foot the posse closed in on what turned out to be the Reynolds gang's campfire. Sparks directed his men to encircle the camp. But apparently one of the men charged in too soon, alerting the gang. With the two groups shooting at each other through the darkness, the gang was able to mount its horses and escape.

Sparks and his posse decided to spend the night at Kenosha House. When they returned to the campsite the next day, they found the body of Owen Singleterry, apparently killed in the crossfire of the previous night. Singleterry had been a top aide to Reynolds. Sparks's posse buried him near the camp, and his knife was stuck in a tree above the grave. The Reynolds gang had scattered in various directions when they fled the night before. Tom Holliman rode to Cañon City. Some of Sparks's posse followed him and easily captured him while he was asleep. Holliman was taken back to Fairplay and jailed.

John Reynolds, Jake Stowe, and John Andrews were pursued south, escaping into New Mexico Territory. Stowe was apparently shot during the Handcart Gulch incident, later dying of his wounds. Andrews was said to have been killed in a saloon brawl in Texas. John Reynolds remained at large and probably fled the territory. Jim Reynolds and three others retreated into the hills. It was unlikely that they would have been able to carry any treasure with them during their hasty retreat.

Two days later, Jim Reynolds and his smaller gang reappeared at a ranch outside of Fairplay. Desperate for food and shelter, they took over the ranch. Sighted by lookouts in the area, Reynolds's band was pursued and barely escaped. A new posse led by Captain George L. Shoup included seventy-five men, supply wagons, and cooks, in order to cover such a wide swath of the search area. The Reynolds gang was unable to outmaneuver this large network. Fleeing southeast of Cañon City, they were finally pinned down. All four men were captured without resistance. Along with Tom Holliman (who had been brought from Fairplay), they were taken to Denver. No portion of the stolen loot was found on the men.

Although Colorado was not officially involved in the Civil War, many residents had sympathies with one side or the other. In Denver, Unionists outnumbered those who favored the Confederacy.

The arrest of the Reynolds gang created a stir in the city, and local officials were concerned that some Southern-leaning locals might attempt to free the five jailed men. To avoid problems, the prisoners were turned over to a local Union military division for protection.

The army apparently held its own trial and found the men guilty of conspiring against the US government. But there was a public outcry that the military had overstepped its authority, and so it was then announced that the prisoners would be taken to Fort Leavenworth, Kansas, to have their case reviewed. The Third Colorado Cavalry under a Captain Cree escorted the five gang members out of Denver.

The next day, the captain and his troops returned to Denver, claiming that the prisoners had all been killed during an escape attempt. A local scout, however, traveling from Fort Leavenworth and passing through the old ghost town of Russellville, found the bodies of five men lashed to trees, all shot to death. Cree later maintained that he had been ordered to kill the men as soon as he could after leaving Denver and that there had never been any intention to deliver them to Fort Leavenworth.

John Reynolds, Jim's brother, is said to have returned to Colorado Territory in 1871. One story suggests that he looked for the buried treasure, but he must have been unsuccessful. He and another outlaw soon took up horse stealing due to lack of funds. When John was mortally wounded in one of the raids, he supposedly drew a map of the treasure's location for his partner. But his partner must also have been unsuccessful since it was reported that he died penniless in Wyoming.

Is there a treasure buried in the foothills outside of Denver? It's possible but remains a mystery. Of the $3,000 to $100,000 the Reynolds gang might have been carrying, the paper script would by now have rotted away, but the gold, silver, and jewelry would be of great value in today's dollars.

Some years ago, a man named Vernon Crow apparently stumbled upon a gravesite in Handcart Gulch. It had an old rusted knife stuck into a tree above it. He also found the remnants of a rough corral and what might have been a lookout point made of stacked rocks. After word got around of his find, treasure hunters swarmed through the area, but nothing was found.

Perhaps someone did uncover the treasure long ago but never spoke of it. Because most people would find it hard to keep such a secret, it is more likely that the gold, silver, and jewels still lie buried under the ground in Handcart Gulch. They are just waiting to be found.

CHAPTER FOUR
THE LOST JOURNEYS OF UTE CHIEF COLOROW

He was known as Colorow, a Spanish derivation of the word Colorado, meaning red, and his skin was said to have been even more red than most of his Ute tribe members. He stood at nearly six feet, unusually tall for Indians of the day. By the time most recorded reports of him appear in early 1860s records, he was known as the chief of one of the Ute lodges that lived among the foothills west of present-day Denver.

We know about some of his adventures, and yet almost nothing overall, considering his life span was about seventy years or a little more. Most of his life is a mystery, since no official or written records were kept by American Indian tribes. And only because his existence intersected with the 1859 gold rush in present-day Colorado and Denver do we know about him at all.

He was born into a civilization that had been nearly the same for thousands of years. His way of life stemmed from the tribal need to follow the buffalo herds for food, clothing, and implements. The carcasses from killing a few bison supplied everything his lodge needed for many months at a time. The Utes were hunter-gatherers and moved from one place to the next as often as every six weeks. Each move included the uprooting of everything they owned, which they either carried or pulled, along with the animals they herded. Nothing was left behind.

Bits and pieces of information collected from mountain men, the early US military, immigrant women's journals, government documents and treaties, and late 1800s newspapers and photographs are what modern historians have used to derive the threads of Colorow's fascinating but mysterious and mostly unknown life. And he became something of a legend among the city-dwelling immigrants of the new primitive town of Denver as they heard of his roaming with his tribe in the nearby foothills near what is now Red Rocks Park, as well as in the White River area of present-day Glenwood Springs.

But what were his lost journeys and unknown life events in between his contact with various new immigrant Americans? His later life would have paralleled the lives of Europeans entering the Rocky Mountains from the east, Spaniards and Mexicans coming up from the south, the French at Bents Fort along the Santa Fe Trail, and other Apache, Kiowa, and Arapaho tribes across the present state of Colorado. Stories tell of his appearance in many locations. How did he live when he was not consorting with the new interlopers into his culture?

The date of Colorow's birth is unknown, but since later Indian reservation records show that he died in 1888, and was estimated to have lived into his seventies, his birth would likely have been around 1818 or earlier. Surprisingly, he was not originally a Ute at all. He was born a Comanche in northern New Mexico.

A common occurrence among Indian tribes was the kidnapping of women and children from the other tribes while warring over horse herds, hunting, or other territorial interactions. When Colorow was a young boy, he was kidnapped by the Utes and brought to Colorado. He grew up in the Colorado foothills near what is now Denver, and never saw his original family again.

We have no way of knowing when he was kidnapped, but likely between age five and ten, since children at that age were expected to help with chores and other work. They were also expected to meld into their new tribe's way of life, and younger children were more likely to accommodate this.

How Colorow grew up in an adopted tribe and became one of its chiefs is another mystery. As an adult, he was considered bright and capable, and his taller-than-average stature also may have contributed to his leadership role. Nothing is known of his years as a young boy among the Utes.

Through stories later related by ranchers, newspapers, early immigrants, and US military personnel, it is said that Colorow married a Ute woman named Re-cha from the Yamparika lodge. The Yampa River is located on the western slope of the Rockies, far from the front-range foothills near present-day Denver, so she must have been a member of that lodge. The fact that she met Colorow suggests that either he had traveled widely around the state by that time or she was brought to him through some migration or other event. Perhaps brides were purposely sought from other lodges to keep their small bands from becoming inbred.

Colorow's Ute name was Too-p'-weets, which meant "rock solid." But all references made in any newspaper or in official documents of that time give his name as Colorow, which is believed to be a mispronunciation of Colorado. And since he was kidnapped from what was present-day New Mexico, the name was possibly derived from the language spoken by Mexican immigrants with whom his early tribe came in contact. No one knows for sure.

Colorow and Re-cha had three children between 1833 and 1842. Their first-born was a daughter named To-pol-ly-wack (1833), followed by a son named Umcompahgre Colorow (1835), and then another son named Pat-cho-or-o-wits or "Gus" (1842). Re-cha was said to have died after falling off a horse when it reared up from being spooked by a bear. Apparently Colorow followed Ute tradition by marrying Re-cha's two sisters. By 1857, the two wives had given birth to nine more children who added to Colorow's growing family.

Some other events are known about Colorow's early life, and about the tribal ways of his people. Although the Utes lived mostly in the foothills, they moved frequently from one encampment to the next, occasionally relocating to the plains south of present-day Denver to hunt the great American bison. These "buffalo" were known to have roamed into the foothills, but hunting them was easier on the open prairie where they could be stampeded over rock cliffs, and more easily skinned and butchered at camps set up right next to the kill sites. The only predator feared by the Utes themselves were the Arapaho Indians who lived in the plains area. The Utes avoided this tribe as much as possible.

It is also unknown how the first encounter may have happened between Chief Colorow and the new immigrants bringing their foreign world of different-looking people with new gadgets, houses built of hewn wood, and wagons that moved on wheels. What an astonishing shock for Colorow and his people to see non-Indian humans suddenly appear onto their once unchanged landscape. The Spanish had filtered into southern present-day Colorado, where they had introduced horses as early as the 1600s, so it is likely that Colorow had some knowledge of other races of humans and their presence in other areas. (His name "Colorow" being of Spanish derivation also certainly suggests some interaction). Given the sheer size of the Utes' land, it's likely the tribe didn't anticipate an intrusion by outsiders. That first meeting must have been stunning. One thing that Chief Colorow came to know for sure is that these new squatters were never going to leave. And they didn't look at the world, or at nature, the same way he did.

From the time that the young boy Colorow was brought to the foothills outside of what is now Denver, in approximately 1825 until approximately 1860, his life and culture had been mostly without outside influences. But as the new immigrants began to intrude into Ute territory, and for the next thirty-eight years until his death, his world would never, ever be the same. He did not assimilate his tribe into this new world, but tried at first to ignore it, and then ultimately to coexist with it. One can only imagine the tumult, the culture shock, and the emotional impact the arrival of white people had on Colorow and his tribe's way of life.

Yet Colorow lived the rest of his life still acting as the Ute chief that he had been trained to be. He journeyed with and without his lodge throughout present-day Colorado, eastern Utah, southern Wyoming, and possibly into New Mexico. No information is known about those journeys, but there are stories told by the early settlers who came to present-day Colorado that he showed up in those various places. We can only speculate.

Many such reports of his whereabouts after 1860 exist because the new American immigrants kept records in journals and public documents. For instance, in 1864, one report mentioned that Colorow showed up at Alex Rooney's ranch between Green Mountain and the hogback ridge near Red Rocks. The Rooneys had just begun to build their ranch house. The gold rush had brought them from Iowa, but ranching began to look like the more productive way to earn a living. Since moving onto this land, they had always been friendly to the Indians. On this particular day, Colorow was with some of his men and a few children. The Rooneys had a red-haired little girl who awed the Utes, who had never seen such bright-colored hair! While the parents stepped away to gather items from their garden, Colorow switched one of his children with the red-haired girl and rode off. After a fearful search by the Rooneys, they finally found their little girl and exchanged the Ute child for her. Reports claim that the Indians found this whole incident to be amusing.

In about 1863 or 1864, another appearance was reported when Chief Colorow was involved in a wrestling match in the San Luis Valley, at Fort Garland. He had wanted to challenge the "chief of the whites." He apparently didn't win.

Also around the same time, stories were told of Chief Colorow stopping in at various newly settled ranches in the foothills outside of Denver. He was interested in the biscuits that the wives baked for their families. He would bring his braves and ask for biscuits to feed all of them. The women often gave him as much as they could, and hoped that he wouldn't linger.

The influx of new immigrants never stopped. The US government began to negotiate for Ute land through treaties, starting with the Tabaguache Treaty of 1863, which began the never-ending string of land-grabbing promises. Although the Utes were paid, it was only the beginning of the desire for more of their land. Colorow was one of the signers of this treaty. In 1868, the Kit Carson Treaty rearranged the Ute boundaries, giving yet more land away. And because land for Ute hunting was being restricted, the US government began to issue rations at various agencies and forts for the Utes to come pick up. The Brunot Treaty of 1873 was one of the largest land negotiations between the US government and the Ute tribe. President Ulysses S. Grant actually traveled to Colorado that year and met with several Ute chiefs, including Colorow, at a reception in Denver on April 28. By September, the treaty was signed and later ratified in Congress in April, 1874. Colorow was one of many signers. The Ute people were not entirely happy about this decision by their leaders, and western slope Ute Chief Ouray's authority was challenged when he was attacked with a knife months before the signing. But it moved forward anyway.

It is known that Colorow continued his travels around the present state of Colorado by using government permits that were issued to him and his tribe for hunting their food instead of receiving rations. And in 1867, one newspaper in Golden, Colorado, the *Colorado Transcript*, reported that a "large delegation" of men and women of the Ute tribe were in town to trade and barter "their furs and skins for flour, sugar, and coffee." Also in the late 1860s,

Utes visited photographers in Central City, Denver, and Colorado Springs to allow their portraits to be taken in exchange for payment. They would then use this money to buy various products at the local stores. Chief Colorow is shown in a photograph in 1873 wearing a black bowler-type hat, which he likely obtained during one of these shopping sprees.

Another enjoyment for Colorow and the Utes was horse racing, a pastime documented quite often in local newspapers in the 1870s. Sometimes the immigrants raced against the Utes. The *Denver Daily Times* reported in 1877 that one of the races was to be against Colorow's winning pony from the previous Saturday's race.

As more immigrants encroached on the Denver area, Colorow's interaction with them increased. New settlers were following the gold veins being reported up in the foothills. Along with the increasing population in the city of Denver was the appearance of the US Cavalry, which began to pressure the Utes. The immigrants wanted land for ranching, and miners were staking claims on land that the Utes always assumed was theirs. Skirmishes and disagreements began to occur between the Utes and the new immigrants. Some incidents were reported that involved Chief Colorow.

Horse racing became one issue that Indian Agent Nathan Meeker, of the White River agency, began to scorn. His view of the Utes was very negative and he complained about them often in letters to authorities in Washington. After Colorow's son Tabernash was shot and killed in 1878 after going back to their old racetrack, tensions heightened, eventually leading to what is termed "The Meeker Massacre" in 1879, when Meeker called for army backup

Chief Colorow

National Anthropological Archives, Smithsonian Institution

and the Utes reacted by killing him. Chief Colorow testified at the later investigation and hearing.

The death of Meeker heightened the rising tensions between the American immigrants and the entire Ute tribe. By 1880, an agreement was made to move the Utes out of Colorado to avoid all-out war. Chief Colorow, now an older man, left the White

River band where he had eventually moved, and now requested movement to the Umcompaghre band. His friend Chief Ouray, Ute leader from the western slope, signed the agreement, against Colorow's recommendation. Ouray died of a long illness just two days later.

The Ute world was coming to an end, and in 1881 the exodus to Utah had begun. Approximately 1,500 Utes, along with thousands of sheep and ponies, were escorted out of Colorado. Chief Colorow stubbornly held back, insistent upon being the very last Ute to leave the valley.

Life in Utah was difficult, and Colorow was still said to be defiant. He often left the reservation and rode into western Colorado, and was just able to keep ahead of soldiers pursuing him on his forays.

One surprising event took place in 1883, after the Umcompaghre Utes had been moved to Utah. The Denver National Mining Exposition invited the lodge to come to Denver to demonstrate western Indian life. In her book *Colorow! A Colorado Photographic Chronicle,* Beth Simmons, PhD, states, "To get to the Queen City of the Plains, the Utes probably rode the train, horses and all, from Rawlins, Wyoming, at the expense of exposition management." Once there, the Utes performed the typical foot and pony races of their culture. And the now famous historical photographer of the west, William Henry Jackson, took photos of the entire Ute delegation. Chief Colorow and many of his family members were among the throng. The Utes were paid for providing the special entertainment at the exhibition with various items of clothing, trinkets, and money. They were likely also fed well.

But by the time of the 1885 census of all US territories, Colorow was listed on the Uintah Reservation. He was an aging man by then, but still ventured into Colorado whenever possible.

In 1887, one more incident involving Colorow was reported nationally, and it was given the name "Colorow's War." In fact, a war against the Utes created this dispute—Colorow and his people did not fight a war at all. Colorado immigrants were unhappy with what they considered to be "trespassing" onto the old reservation by the Utes, and they decided to burn all the old buildings there without giving the tribe any warning. Although the Utes had come back there on one of their journeys, they were not planning to stay. Most of their possessions were lost in the fires, and they were soon on the run. Eventually the Buffalo Soldiers came to the Utes' rescue, and they were escorted back to Utah.

In late 1888, Chief Colorow died of pneumonia. Though many would see his death as his final surrender, modern historians view Colorow's life as one of heroic proportions. He led his people during one of the most tumultuous upheavals of any culture in history, against impossible odds.

So much mystery remains, including the gap of forty or more years from his approximate birth in 1818 to around 1860, when almost nothing is known about how he lived or his journeys throughout the Rocky Mountains. It was said that he knew every trail along the foothills, and over the mountains, and through all the river valleys in the vicinity of present-day Colorado and borders of neighboring states. We know about his kidnapping and later marriages and that he had children. All this took place while his culture was living solidly in its traditions without outside influence. But his remaining life, after the influx of the American immigrants, lasted about thirty years. What we know of him during that time period is based on several anecdotes, newspaper clippings, photographs, and military reports. Fortunately, this information allows us to know how Chief Colorow played such a significant role in the last days of the Ute civilization, while it was still an independent nation. These accounts have all contributed to the legend of Colorow.

For as little as is known about him, this Ute chief made a big impression in the later historical record of the state of Colorado. Many locations have been named after him: Colorow's Inspiration Tree and Colorow Point Park (which was designated as a Denver City mountain park in 1915) are both in Jefferson County; Colorow Hill and Colorow Road are located on Lookout Mountain overlooking Denver; Morrison has a Colorow Drive and Colorow Cave; and Littleton is home to Colorow Elementary School and the adjoining Chief Colorow Park, as well as a Colorow Water Station.

CHAPTER FIVE
P. T. BARNUM

There's a sign at the entrance to a neighborhood on the west side of Denver: WELCOME TO BARNUM.

As in P. T. Barnum? The famous promoter and circus owner from the 1800s? Did he actually have something to do with Denver?

Legends abound. Ask around among the locals, and you'll get all sorts of answers: "Oh, yes, P. T. Barnum lived here a long time ago." Or, "His winter quarters for the circus were just up the road." Or maybe, "I think he owned a horse ranch south of Denver." Someone else might say, "P. T. Barnum and Horace Greeley founded a town together in Colorado." And yet another person might maintain, "Barnum lived right over on King Street—I've been on a tour of his home. He built a sanitarium next to the Capitol too." Their neighbor might add, "I heard a story that Barnum got the land for the Barnum neighborhood as a gift from an Indian chief."

These stories go on and on.

So are any of these stories true? Much mystery surrounds whether P. T. Barnum lived in Colorado and whether he had any connection with this state at all.

Phineas Taylor Barnum was born in Bethel, Connecticut, on July 5, 1810, one of five children. He grew up on the eastern seaboard and according to his official biographies lived there all his life. Was Colorado ever a part of his story?

Barnum had spent his early life becoming one of the most successful and outlandish promoters of his time. At the age of twenty-five, he came across a woman named Joyce Heth who claimed to be 161 years old and to have been a nurse to George Washington. Barnum paid Heth $1,000 to tell her story to audiences he attracted with handbills. He took the show throughout New York and New England and supposedly earned $1,500 per week from it.

In 1841 Barnum bought Scudder's American Museum on Broadway in New York. Here he presented "500,000 natural and artificial curiosities from every corner of the globe." Year after year, he came up with entertaining, yet often preposterous, shows. Always purported to be true, the actual origin of many of Barnum's "real" and "genuine" exhibits was subject to question. In 1842 "The Feejee Mermaid" (a supposedly embalmed mermaid found near Calcutta) attracted throngs. And 1842 was also the year that he exhibited Tom Thumb to paying crowds, including, at one point, England's Queen Victoria.

Barnum could promote anything. He knew how to draw people in and make them want to come back for more. And so when Jenny Lind, the budding European opera star, needed an American promoter in 1850, Barnum was the right choice. Promoting Lind's ninety-five concerts, Barnum made her famous as "The Swedish Nightingale."

In 1854 he published his autobiography, writing of a lifetime of adventures and events. Yet he was still only forty-four years old.

In 1870 he created a circus that he billed as "The Greatest Show on Earth!" A typical spread of tents and attractions took up as much as five acres and drew audiences of 10,000 people. Because this circus traveled by train all across the United States, nearly every American alive in the late 1800s had a chance to see this fantastic show of animal and human performers. Although P. T. Barnum was already well known, the circus made him a household name.

Records show that Barnum's circus did in fact come to Denver in 1880, 1895, and 1905. But while posters advertising the event claimed that the "great showman P. T. Barnum" was coming, he never actually appeared in Colorado with his circus.

Barnum apparently first became interested in Colorado while attending a meeting in New York City on Christmas Eve, 1869. He was fifty-nine years old. He had great admiration for the newspaperman Horace Greeley, and Greeley wanted to establish an agricultural colony on land in northeastern Colorado. Given the temperance sentiments in the country at the time, the community would be liquor free. Greeley was calling his plan Union Colony No. 1. Barnum and many others who were looking for a place to invest their wealth were enthusiastic. Although Barnum hadn't seen the site, he became a charter member of this not-yet-born city in Colorado. (It would later be called Greeley.)

Still, he had no plans to set foot in Colorado. His daughter, however, would play a large part in changing that. Helen, one of Barnum's four daughters, had just gone through a scandalous

Despite having a neighborhood in west Denver named after him, famous promoter and entertainer P. T. Barnum only visited Colorado four times.

divorce in Indiana. She'd fallen in love with a man named William Buchtel, an alcoholic physician with tuberculosis.

Barnum wasn't pleased about Helen's divorce and the scandal that went with it, nor did he approve of her choice of a new fiancé.

But Barnum loved his daughter and wanted to help her begin a new life away from Indiana. Helen and William were soon married there and left immediately afterward for Union Colony No. 1. Not only would the move give them a fresh start, but Barnum thought the "dry town" would help William with his drinking problem.

When P. T. Barnum made his first plans to visit Colorado, it was to take a look at his investment but mainly to visit his daughter and husband. He arrived in Denver in 1870 on a stagecoach from Cheyenne. He had just lectured there and was now scheduled to speak in Denver, Georgetown, and the new colony. The title of the lecture was "How to Be Healthy, Happy and Rich."

He also became interested in what else the state might have to offer. Always interested in places to invest, Barnum looked into buying more Colorado real estate. This is where some of the stories surrounding Barnum originate.

Did Barnum build several buildings in Colorado called Barnum's Block?

Yes! Barnum's daughter Helen and her husband did not live in Greeley long. But while they were there, they ran a large hotel that had been built with Barnum's money. He also built a few more buildings in the same location in the early 1870s, and they became known as Barnum's Block. But William's drinking problem undermined any success. He had started selling wine secretly from his pharmacy on the block. Soon the teetotaler citizens demanded that he and Helen leave town. They packed their bags and went to Denver.

Did P. T. Barnum really build a sanitarium in Denver?

Yes, he did. Still hoping to help his daughter, Barnum found land in Denver near what was then called Brown's Bluff. The bluff would soon be the site for the new capitol building. Barnum's property (between Seventeenth and Eighteenth Streets along Sherman and Lincoln) became prime real estate. Since William had tuberculosis and was doing much better in the dry Denver climate, Barnum and his son-in-law worked together to build a sanitarium where other sufferers could come and recover. It was called Prospect Villa and opened in 1873. It was located just a couple of blocks from the Capitol. Unfortunately, the venture did not succeed.

Did he own any other large tracts of property in Colorado?

Indeed, he also invested in about 10,000 acres for a ranch that he called Hermosilla in Huerfano County in southern Colorado. A partner of Barnum's thought this dry area would be suitable for cattle. Barnum apparently was never convinced of this idea but went in on the venture anyway. He owned the property from 1871 until 1877 and then sold out to his partner.

Is there really a town near Denver named after P. T. Barnum?

Yes. It was once a separate town, but it is now a neighborhood within the city limits of Denver. In 1878 Barnum bought this hilly tract of land intending for it to be developed into fashionable homes with views of both downtown Denver and the mountains to the west. Helen and her husband lived in the Villa Park section of Barnum, and William was even its mayor for three years. Unfortunately, water was not readily available and P. T.'s grand designs fizzled. He finally gave the property to his daughter Helen in 1884. She bequeathed it to her own daughter, Leila Buchtel. Its boundaries are Alameda Avenue on the south, Sheridan Street on the west,

Sixth Avenue on the north, and Federal Street on the east. The Villa Park neighborhood to the north of Sixth Avenue was also a part of the original property.

Did an Indian chief give the real estate for the town of Barnum to P. T. Barnum as a gift?

No. This is a good story but an urban legend. Supposedly, P. T. Barnum met an Indian chief who told him that, in a dream, he'd seen Barnum giving him a white horse as a gift. Barnum replied that he'd had a dream too, and in the dream the chief had given Barnum the large tract of land they were standing on. When P. T. Barnum came back later with the white horse and gave it to the Indian chief, the chief gave the land to Barnum.

In reality Barnum was a member of the Villa Park Association, which bought the property, and he in turn bought it from them.

And contrary to rumors, P. T. Barnum never ever actually lived in Colorado. He had investments and property only. Due in part to misinformed (or ill-intentioned) tour guides, many have been led to believe that P. T. Barnum had a home at 360 King Street in the Barnum neighborhood. One local huckster might even have been championed by P. T. Barnum himself for his ability to convince people of this fable! And the largest home in the Barnum neighborhood, 325 King Street? Again, despite the rumors, it had nothing to do with Barnum or his daughter. The home was built in the late 1800s by a local architect and is now used as a school for boys.

And what about Circus Town? Did Barnum ever use some part of Colorado as a winter headquarters for his circus?

No. Although Colorado weather is often quite comfortable in the winter, it still would not be suitable for circus animals.

During one of his visits, Barnum was said to have remarked that the dry air and warm sunny days would make a fine climate to winter his animals, but it never went further. More recently, a pamphlet about the Jefferson County Open Space Parks mentions that a board was said to be found in a home at Meyers Ranch Park saying Circus Town 1889. It is one version of an often-told story but is nevertheless still false.

Another legendary story, which even appears in recently published books on Colorado, suggests that Barnum's circus appeared in the high mountain town of Breckenridge. To travel there, the train would have needed to cross Boreas Pass west of Fairplay. The legend says that the train could not make the steep grade, and so the elephants were taken off the train to help push it up the mountain (somewhat like the elephants pushing Hannibal's wagons over the mountains in ancient Europe). But there is no evidence that Barnum's circus ever appeared in Breckenridge.

Finally, any report on P. T. Barnum would be incomplete without at least one truly outlandish hoax. In the East, for instance, he'd presented the "Cardiff Giant" as an enormous petrified man, excavated by a local farmer. In fact, the artifact had been manufactured out of cement. Similarly, in Colorado, the Solid Muldoon hoax was based on another manufactured fossil, passed off as the petrified body of an ancient man. Barnum claimed that it had been found in Colorado, near his Huerfano ranch. Real bones had been inserted to fool investigators, and in fact some scientists were convinced it was real. But eastern newspapers, aware of the old Cardiff Giant scheme, remained skeptical. Barnum finally sold the hoax to "Soapy" Smith in Creede, Colorado. Soapy was a Colorado conman in his own right, and when he got hold of the Solid Muldoon, he changed the name to Colonel Stone and exhibited it with much fanfare, even conducting "educational" lectures about fossils. It was a great success.

P. T. Barnum actually visited Colorado only four times, in 1870, 1872, 1877, and 1890. During his short visits, he became involved in so many diverse projects that the legends about him grew disproportionately. More than a hundred years after his death, the Ringling Bros. and Barnum & Bailey Circus still carries his name, and a neighborhood in west Denver does, too. And the stories about him living in Colorado still linger.

He died in 1891 at the age of eighty-one, but not before reading his own obituary. He had complained that newspapers only write nice things about people after they die. The *New York Sun* responded by publishing his obituary on the front page a few weeks before his death. Nothing was mentioned about Colorado. Showman until the end, he planned his own funeral and was laid to rest in Bridgeport, Connecticut.

CHAPTER SIX

LOUIS DUPUY AND THE HOTEL DE PARIS

"The mysterious Frenchman" is the moniker many used to describe this new resident of the mountain mining town of Georgetown, Colorado. Like so many other immigrants to America in the early 1870s, Louis Dupuy had come to start a new life. Sometimes this meant leaving the Old World behind, including essential facts of one's former life. It was often preferable to forget the past.

His name was pronounced "Lu-wee Du-pwee" in the language of his homeland of France. For his new friends in this rough new country where English was predominant, his name rolled off their tongues easily and sounded very exotic. Louis Dupuy would soon find this helpful in designing his new image.

The young Dupuy had found a job in Denver as a reporter and was sent to Georgetown to write about its mining boom for the *Rocky Mountain News*. Its publisher, William Byers, had noticed Dupuy's abilities and wondered how he had become so well educated. But Dupuy remained mute about his past. And although Dupuy benefited from Byers's notice, it would later be Byers who would benefit from this connection with Dupuy. The mystery had already begun. Instantly likeable, Dupuy made friends easily. The

Georgetown locals not only noted his French accent but also his way with words. He was a gentleman, charming and refined. Many wondered how he had acquired such style, though Louis Dupuy did not offer any details. And, like others in town who wanted to share in the wealth of the silver industry, he caught "mining fever." Dupuy soon left his reporter's job and began working in Georgetown's Cold Stream Mine, hauling ore from the earth.

Georgetown had grown into one of the finer cities in Colorado. With a population of more than 5,000, some of the streets were lined with Victorian mansions. It had an opera house, parks, fine shops, and four fire stations, and the steeples of several churches rose above the rooftops.

The mysterious Frenchman labored hard in the mines. And in 1873, when dynamite was accidentally detonated in the Kennedy Tunnel section of the Cold Stream Mine, Dupuy was said to have saved a friend's life by pushing him out of the full force of the blast. But Louis sustained broken bones and was badly injured in the mishap.

While he lay convalescing for many weeks, Dupuy rethought his life. What should he do when he recovered? Mining had lost its appeal, but he wanted to stay in Georgetown and would need to provide for himself. He began to envision an extraordinary plan. He would build and operate a hotel! But it would not be an ordinary hotel. He told his friend and physician, Dr. R. D. Collins, "In this land of gold and silver, people should live like princes. We should have a great hostelry and the best of wines. While we cannot have the masterpieces of Michelangelo and Cellini, we can at least have the reproductions. I would have a library and the thoughts of the best authors of the Old World would be upon its shelves."

The town of Georgetown was not only progressive, it had a heart as well. A public subscription was solicited whereby citizens donated funds to help the heroic and injured Louis Dupuy. These funds, along with new income he would earn working as a cook in a bakery, allowed him to begin his dream. He rented a building that had formerly housed the Delmonico bakery on Alpine Street (now Sixth Street). It was a two-story frame building with a dining room in front, a kitchen in back, and four bedrooms upstairs.

He labored for months to remodel the building. The stone, brick, and cabinet work was done mostly by Dupuy himself. A French woodcarver and Italian craftsmen helped him with the finer touches. On October 9, 1875, the Hotel de Paris opened its doors to the public. It offered steam heat, unheard of in the mountains. Hot and cold water was available in each room, elegant carpets adorned the floors, and pretty place settings tastefully graced the tables in the dining room. A large French bake oven had been bought for the kitchen. And furnishings were imported from Europe and New York, brought by ship to this continent, then by steam trains to Denver, and by wagon to Georgetown.

The hotel was an immediate success. But Louis Dupuy was only getting started. The mystery of his past broadened when it was learned that he was also a fine French chef, and he personally cooked all the meals for the patrons in the restaurant.

The menu for one evening was as follows:

Oysters on the Half Shell

Soup

Ptarmigan or Pheasant in Casserole

Venison Cutlet

Sweet Breads Eugenie

Apple Fritters

Salad

French Bread

Peach Charlotte with Brandy Sauce

Petit Fours

Fine Wines

Coffee

Over the next twenty-five years, as he developed the Hotel de Paris into one of the most exquisite hotels in the country, he also gained a reputation for his French cuisine and distinguished wine cellar. These fine wines of Europe were shipped in wooden casks and Louis bottled them himself. But how could a young man, whose only known occupations had been as a reporter and miner, be so adept at running such a fine hotel and restaurant?

New perspectives about this man were revealed as he shared more of his talents as proprietor of this glorious hotel in Georgetown. Guests marveled and wondered about him. He could regale them with discussions of the great philosophers, religion, politics, and science.

Colorado's Georgetown, like many mining communities, attracted a diversity of residents, including "the mysterious Frenchman," Louis Dupuy.

He also tantalized them by sharing small glimpses of his life, saying that he had once squandered a large inheritance. And that he had served in the French army. But Dupuy continued to remain coy about his early life.

Louis Dupuy and the Hotel de Paris were practically synonymous. He lived there, worked there, and socialized there. He was constantly enlarging and improving it. Some thought that he perhaps embellished what stories he did reveal of his early life, but there was no doubt about the reality of his fabulous embellishments to the hotel. It was gradually enlarged to include eight bedrooms. He hung fine paintings on the walls and installed a beautiful black walnut and silver maple floor in the dining room. An ornate French fountain was placed there as well. A pool held small brook trout that Dupuy cooked for his guests.

Rooms were added specifically to be used by salesmen to display their wares. Ornate mantelpieces were carved from walnut, and "diamond dust" mirrors were installed, fabricated to have a smoky look.

More rooms were added, including bathrooms that featured the latest conveniences such as tubs, water closets, and elevated flush tanks. Louis Dupuy built his own quarters with a bedroom, library, and bath. Outside adornments included statues of a sitting stag deer, a lion, and Justice holding a set of scales.

After the next-door McClellan Opera House burned in 1892, Dupuy used the exposed wall of the hotel to paint an elaborate design of crossed American and French flags, and the name, "Hotel

DENVER PUBLIC LIBRARY, WESTERN HISTORY COLLECTION, OTTO ROACH, X-1101

The dining room in Louis Dupuy's Hotel de Paris was one of the most luxurious in the West, accoutered with linen tablecloths, china from Limoge, France, and a wooden floor made from alternating stripes of silver maple and black walnut.

De Paris." Electric lights were added to the hotel in 1893. According to the *American Heritage Cookbook*, Dupuy's "premises made culinary history throughout the West. Many visiting celebrities made pilgrimages to Georgetown aboard the red-plush coaches of the narrow gauge Colorado Central railroad to sample gourmet food at the Hotel de Paris, and to engage in literary conversations with Louis, an eccentric of engaging dimensions."

One of the "celebrities" referred to was William Byers, Dupuy's former boss and owner of the *Rocky Mountain News*. Now it was Byers who received the attention of the famous hotelier.

The Hotel de Paris continued to thrive and remained popular throughout Dupuy's life. It afforded him additional pleasures in spite of its constant demands on his time. He had purchased a ranch near Hot Sulphur Springs in 1888 and enjoyed this getaway whenever he could. And he traveled back to France in 1897. This was the only time he revisited his homeland. Unfortunately, there is no record of what he did there. This would likely have enlightened historians with answers to the myriad questions that still remain about him.

Louis Dupuy died of pneumonia in 1900, at the age of fifty-six. He had not been sickly, and some thought the illness may have been precipitated by the cold baths he insisted on taking as a health measure!

It would not be until after his death that some of the puzzles of his life would be exposed. Dupuy's closest friends in Georgetown were his physician, Dr. R. D. Collins, his lawyer, John J. White, and the editor of the *Georgetown Courier*, Jessie Randall. Between them they began to create a more complete picture of the famous hotelier and restaurateur.

Louis Dupuy's Hotel de Paris as it stands today.

They revealed that Louis Dupuy's real name was Adolphe Francois Gerard. He was born on October 14, 1844, in Alencon, France, in the department of Orne (a region known for its lace). His parents were Pierre Auguste Aubey and Marie Claire Jacquine Aubey. His father, Pierre, was a modest innkeeper and he died when Adolphe was just a year old. His mother remarried in 1850, and both she and Adolphe took her new husband's surname, Gerard.

Young Adolphe was sent away to school at the age of fifteen because his mother had wanted him to become a priest. He attended the Catholic seminary in Saez and was taught literature and languages. But in 1864, at the age of twenty, he became disenchanted with the rigid discipline and left the school. He went to Paris, where he washed dishes in a cafe before finding a job as an apprentice chef in a large Paris hotel. He worked there for a year, learning to prepare fine French cuisine. But he was still restless and left Paris.

He is said to have wanted to improve his English, and perhaps he was already thinking about America. As a first step he went to London, finding a job as a newspaper writer and translator. In 1868 he finally set foot in New York City.

Dupuy took whatever odd jobs he could. Perhaps because jobs were scarce (or maybe because of some trouble that he was said to have had over copying another's work), he soon enlisted in the army. He was sent to Fort Riley, Kansas, then to Cheyenne, Wyoming. Not surprisingly, he found himself unsuited to army life. Less than a year after enlisting, he deserted and changed his name. He hoped that he would not be pursued among the crowds of immigrants when he went to Denver.

Now in Colorado's capital city, he took a job delivering papers. As "Louis Dupuy" he submitted some articles to the *Rocky Mountain News* about the French politics of the day. The owner of the paper offered him a job writing about the silver boom in the mountains. For the next year Dupuy traveled all over the state, visiting mining camps such as Breckenridge and Silver Plume.

But it was Georgetown that most attracted Louis Dupuy, and he settled there. It was a decision that would propel him into one of the most amazing lives in Colorado.

Many mysteries still remain about Louis Dupuy. There is no evidence that he'd ever had the opportunity to squander an inheritance. Additionally, no records show that he was ever in the French army. And was there ever romance in his life? One reference to a young woman named Ada Bryant suggests that she may have been a love interest. She was of French descent and lived in Georgetown. Her health was delicate and Louis provided her with healthy food.

She was a devout Catholic, however, and Louis was said to have become an agnostic or atheist. Records show that she later married A. D. Barnes in 1877.

One woman had lived in close proximity to Dupuy during all the years he ran the hotel. He left his hotel and all his property to Sophie Gally, a French housekeeper who had lived in a small room on the second floor of his hotel. She was about ten years older than Dupuy, and he had always referred to her as his "guest," but there is no evidence to suggest that she was anything more to him than an employee. She died four months after Dupuy, and the hotel was left to her relatives in France, who then sold it to a local resident, Sara Burkholder. She preserved the character of the hotel and almost all of the furnishings for the next fifty-four years while she ran it as a hotel and later rented it as a residence. In 1954 the Colonial Dames of America bought the hotel and have preserved it as a museum to this day.

Louis Dupuy would undoubtedly be pleased that his "souvenir of France," the name he often called his hotel, is still both intact and revered for its finery and artifacts. And while many of his secrets have been exposed, he would likely be quite content to know that much about his life remains unknown. He continues to be "the mysterious Frenchman."

CHAPTER SEVEN
THE MOTHER
CABRINI SHRINE

In 1912 a devout Catholic nun from Italy came to the dry foothills near Golden, Colorado. She was there to help establish a camp for girls on property that was both available and affordable. Professionals had been summoned to help find a viable water source but concluded that none existed. The local sisters confided this to their visitor. The nun, Mother Frances Xavier Cabrini, walked with the sisters among the rocky terrain and pondered the problem. She soon pointed and said, "Lift that rock over there and dig." The sisters obeyed and soon uncovered a spring bubbling up with clean water. It has provided this site with all the water needed to this day, never wavering due to drought or low rainfall. Many call what happened that day a miracle. Others call it a mystery. How was Mother Cabrini able to find this spring when no one else could? And who was she? What was her life like, allowing her confidently to bring water into existence in such an arid place? What was the mystery of her life that spawned such a miracle?

Before her life's work came to an end in 1917, Mother Cabrini had accomplished so much and was revered by so many, that the Roman Catholic church subsequently honored her with canonization. She was the first American citizen to become a Catholic saint. Sainthood is bestowed on very few and is not usually achieved for centuries following a person's death. Mother Cabrini, however, was so heralded that the first step of the process, the beatification, took place in 1938; Pope Pius XII signed the decree for her canonization in 1944; and she became a saint at a ceremony in the Vatican in 1946. In his address, Cardinal Samuel Stritch said, "Her life was filled with difficulties . . . many were her disappointments. It was a struggle. Most of the time she had tasks which were far from congenial. At times she was misunderstood even by good people."

He also said, "Our Saint issues a challenge to each of us. Our works in life may be modest, our achievements in the eyes of men insignificant . . . [but] the trials can be blessings, and no matter how gloomy the world about us may be, we can smile the serene smile of our Saint."

When her "banner of the new saint" was carried into the Basilica, 40,000 people were there to applaud the event.

Eventually three shrines were dedicated to Mother Cabrini in the United States—in New York, in Chicago, and on the mountaintop above Golden where the camp for girls had been established, near her "miracle spring."

Frances Cabrini was born July 15, 1850, in Sant'Angelo, Italy. She was the tenth of eleven children born to Agostino Cabrini and Stella Odini. Only four of their children survived into adulthood. Although religious education was repressed in the harsh political climate of the time, Frances persisted in her education at Catholic schools and was impressed by her teachers.

By the time she was thirteen years old, she knew that she wanted to be a missionary. She asked to become a member of the Daughters of the Sacred Heart, the order that ran her school. In one of the many rejections she would face in her life, she was turned down. She accepted this defeat but didn't give up her plans. After her parents died and after she was again turned down in her application to a special order, she became a teacher. Soon she would be asked by the bishop to oversee a diocesan girls' orphanage because he felt she was the only one capable. Reluctantly she took the position, once again putting her own desires aside. By the time she was thirty years old in 1880, she had been asked to establish the Missionary Sisters of the Sacred Heart of Jesus. She was still hoping to go out into the world on her mission. In the meantime the education and care of orphans were her primary functions. She went on to establish two more institutes, training young novices along the way.

Frances wanted to establish an institute in Rome, setting it up with a missionary focus. Her plans were almost thwarted again, however, when the archbishop asked her to stay near home. She insisted on Rome, although she had never traveled so far away before. She ultimately founded not one, but two orphanages in the city. She soon met Bishop Giovanni Scalabrini, the founder of the Missionaries of St. Charles. He needed her in America to help Italian immigrants. Having decided that her missionary destiny was in China, she acquiesced to go to New York reluctantly, intending to work there establishing orphanages for only a short time.

But Pope Leo XIII had other ideas for Frances. By now her establishment of so many institutes in her role with the Missionary

In 1912, Mother Frances Xavier Cabrini, the first American citizen to become a Catholic saint, miraculously discovered water on a dry Colorado hillside.

Sisters of the Sacred Heart was quite impressive. The pope asked her to make her mission in America, not China.

After 1890 and until the end of her life, she visited cities all over America in order to establish orphanages and other institutions to benefit the poor. In August 1902 Bishop Matz of Denver invited Mother Cabrini to open a school mission near his city. Upon her first visit to Denver, Mother Cabrini wrote, "The diocese of Denver comprises a large territory, being the only one in Colorado. The area of this state exceeds that of Italy. One-third of the land is plain whilst two-thirds comprise the mountainous regions of the Rocky Mountains.

"In Denver I have visited the Rocky Mountains. Some of the peaks are more than 14,400 feet high and their peaks are covered with perpetual snow.

"I am so happy to have a mission in the Rocky Mountains where I have always desired to go—may God be blessed!"

Mother Cabrini established many schools, orphanages, and hospitals in Colorado. Most were originally created to help poor Italian immigrants, but over time these same institutes also helped other children and immigrants.

The Mount Carmel school was opened by Mother Cabrini in November 1902, on Navajo Street in Denver. Mother Cabrini wrote, "The Bishop is enthusiastic and I believe it will be one of our nicest missions."

Her enthusiasm for her work was reflected in more journal entries. She wrote,"On Monday, November 18, 1902, the Denver house was inaugurated. . . .We opened a school at once, to which two hundred children came the very first day."

Later, in 1905, Mother Cabrini wrote, "I am amidst the mountains of Colorado. In this splendid state, which is named as they say after its multi-colored mountains, there are flowers and birds of the most brilliant and variegated colors. Let us thank God, who allows such rays of the infinite beauty and power to fall on this earth."

Mother Cabrini also visited various mining areas. In 1906 she wrote, "As the train enters the heart of the mountain district, the locomotive ascends slowly and we are able to admire the beauty of the landscape. Every minute the view changes. We behold austere mountains whose summits are whitened with shining snow, hills quite green with pine trees and reddened by the colours of the rock and soil. Sharp peaks which seem to touch the sky and on which the eagle alone rests."

Mother Cabrini also visited Colorado Springs and Trinidad. She was awed by Pikes Peak and also wrote of the mountain goats, buffalo, and black bears.

Her connection to nature was obviously heightened while she was in Colorado. She wrote, "Here and there silver streams descend among the rocks and soon become threatening torrents which, in rapids and waterfalls, follow their beds of many colored rocks. The name Colorado was never better applied than to this enchanting country, to these most beautiful natural parks, where the hand of man could never add greater beauty than that with which Nature has enriched it. In Truth, Here one Exclaims Spontaneously: How wonderful is God in His Works."

In 1909, while in Seattle, Washington, Mother Cabrini took her oath of allegiance to the United States of America and became a new citizen. Her mission had now become entirely focused on helping the immigrants who came to America. They chose to become citizens in their new home, and she decided to join them.

On August 7, 1909, Mother Cabrini and two other sisters took a short trip out of Denver to the foothills several miles away. They drove a horse and buggy toward Golden and went up into Mount Vernon Canyon to look at property. There was an abandoned ranch with three buildings, including a stone barn. Mother Cabrini was warned that the place was completely dry, which was why the property was inexpensive. She decided to buy the property.

A year later, in 1910, she purchased a second tract of adjacent land, and acquired a third parcel in 1912. The fourth parcel was bought much later, in 1934, after Mother Cabrini had died.

On November 15, 1912, she and a group hired a horse and buggy and headed for the property that would eventually be known as the Mother Cabrini Shrine. She had written in a recent letter: "I want Colorado to be one of my best missions." The group enjoyed a picnic lunch together and then climbed up to the top of the mountain. She was impressed by the grand view, overlooking Denver. Inspired, she asked the other sisters to gather as many white quartz rocks as they could find. She used them to shape a heart on the ground, and atop the heart, she shaped a cross. This mountain became known as the Mount of the Sacred Heart, and the heart she created can still be viewed today.

When they had descended the mountain and sat resting, the sisters discussed the problem of having no clean water. Mother Cabrini walked around the small gulch and pointed to a location under a red rock where they would find the "miracle spring." This was her last visit to Colorado.

Mother Cabrini died in Chicago in 1917, at the age of sixty-seven. In 1928 Monsignor Della Chioppa was sent from Rome to visit the spring as part of the process for Mother Cabrini's candidacy for canonization. The miracle of the spring, as well as healing work that she had performed in Chicago and New York, was the basis for her candidacy.

After Mother Cabrini's canonization a committee was formed to establish the Mother Cabrini Shrine in Mount Vernon Canyon. In 1954 a stairway of 373 steps was installed to lead to the top of the Mount of the Sacred Heart. Along the way would be the Stations of the Cross and the fifteen Mysteries of the Rosary. A grotto chapel was built in 1959, and carillon bells were installed in 1961. A large statue was placed at the top of the Mount of the Sacred Heart. Twenty-three feet tall, it depicts Jesus Christ with his sacred heart exposed. It can be seen for miles and is lighted at night, a landmark to this present day.

At the base of the stairway lies the spring. For many years its abundant water filled a big trough, and locals watered their ponies there. Eventually, the spring was housed in a nicer compartment with faucets added for the convenience of visitors. A large holding tank was still needed to hold the overflow. Adolph Coors III, whose brewery was located just down the hill, offered an 8,000-gallon tank if someone could come and pick it up. The National Guard at Camp George West was also located nearby and willingly transported the tank up to the spring. (In another mystery of the time, Adolph Coors III was kidnapped and murdered just one week later, as he drove from Golden to his rural home.)

Mother Cabrini established more than sixty-seven missions, schools, and hospitals for the Missionary Sisters of the Sacred Heart of Jesus. As the first American-citizen saint, she left behind a legacy of prolific works in caring for her fellow humans. And she also left a miracle that remains a mystery to this day. Her "miracle spring" still produces clear water from a place where none should exist.

CHAPTER EIGHT
BUFFALO BILL'S GRAVESITE

A marker on Buffalo Bill's gravesite on Lookout Mountain near Denver reads, IN MEMORIAM. COLONEL WILLIAM FREDERICK CODY. "BUFFALO BILL." NOTED SCOUT AND INDIAN FIGHTER. BORN FEBRUARY 26, 1846, SCOTT COUNTY, IOWA. DIED JANUARY 10, 1917, DENVER, COLORADO. A separate marker reads, AT REST HERE BY HIS REQUEST.

That volatile last sentence lit the fuse on a controversy that is still sputtering today. Perhaps Buffalo Bill was now at peace, but nobody else was—not if they had any thoughts about where his burial site should be located. Since Buffalo Bill led an adventurous life of national and foreign travel and celebrity, how could any one location claim him for his final resting place? But at least three places did. Which one was really "by his own request"?

William Frederick Cody was born in Le Claire, Iowa, in 1846. His family called him "Will," but he grew up being called "Billy" by friends. In the military he became "Bill," then "the Colonel" in his Wild West Show, but the world would eventually dub him "Buffalo Bill."

Cody grew up in a time that his later Wild West Show would illustrate. He played with Indians as a child in Iowa and later in

Kansas where his family moved when he was eight. His father died of scarlet fever when he was eleven. To help provide for his family, young Will became a messenger, cattle herder, and wagon train driver. By the age of fourteen, he was a rider for the Pony Express at Julesburg, Colorado.

Two years later he joined up with the Seventh Kansas Calvary to fight in the Civil War. His family had been strong abolitionists, and he fought for the Union. He served honorably, and the end of the war brought him back to the West. By the time he was eighteen years old, illness had caused the deaths of his sister, both brothers, and his mother and father. He promised to take care of the sisters who were left.

At twenty-one he became chief buffalo hunter and scout for the Kansas Pacific Railroad. His job was to hunt and kill enough buffalo to feed the 1,200 workers who were laying rails across the country. It was said that he killed 4,000 buffalo in one year (about eleven per day). He could outshoot, outride, and outguide anyone. Scouts of that era dressed with long hair, feathers, and bright clothes to distinguish themselves. One friend said, "He went on fourteen different Indian expeditions and never lost his scalp." The US Congress awarded him the Medal of Honor for Acts of Bravery. His reputation grew, and soon European businessmen sought him out to be their guide on hunting excursions.

Legends say that it is true that he killed thousands of buffalo, but some also say that he was single-handedly responsible for their near extinction. Of the estimated sixty million buffalo that roamed the prairie, Bill Cody's share was small. Nevertheless, with his toll added together with the toll of other hunters, hide hunters, and opportunists, the buffalo's numbers declined drastically. Paradoxically, though, Cody would later help to rescue the few buffalo that remained and protect them from extinction.

Bill Cody's name was soon replaced with the moniker "Buffalo Bill." And in 1869 dime-novel author Ned Buntline began making that name famous in his stories of the West. They were full of Old West "half-truths and whole lies." Many legends about Buffalo Bill came straight from these books. Buntline's heroes almost always busted broncos, roped steers, killed buffalo, and fought Indians who always lost the battles.

At the age of twenty-seven, capitalizing on Buntline's successful books about him, Buffalo Bill entered show business. People loved to see him on the theater stage. Throngs came to see him perform in his western costumes, acting out improbable adventures of the West. The real West was dying away, but audiences were crowding in to see these reenactments.

Meanwhile, Buffalo Bill had married, and he and his wife were raising a son and daughter. Since he was nearly always away from home, he had to be reached by telegram to learn that his family had been struck by scarlet fever. He traveled home to North Platte, Nebraska, to find that his five-year-old son, Kit (named for his friend Kit Carson), had died. Bill and his wife were grief stricken.

He returned to the stage but was recalled to go fight the Indians at Warbonnet Creek, Nebraska. There he killed Yellow Hand, a Cheyenne chief, and took his scalp. This time he returned to the stage a hero, and his shows were sellouts. Real life was being portrayed in Saturday matinees just a few weeks after the actual events had taken place!

By 1883, during a visit to Nebraska for the Fourth of July, he came up with an idea for an outdoor Old West exhibition and entertained the people of North Platte that day. It was a resounding success and from this show his famous Wild West Show was launched.

Although Buffalo Bill had killed Indians in many battles, he also made many Indian friends. They gave him the honorary name of Pahaska, meaning "long hair." Many of them joined his Wild West Show, featuring real buffalo, horses, stagecoaches, and authentically presented cowboy and Indian battles. Sitting Bull and Annie Oakley became part of the show, along with champion lasso ropers, Mexican vaqueros, and trick riders. The Old West came alive for his audiences, and the queen of England became one of Buffalo Bill's biggest fans when she attended his show in London. One person even remarked that he had "out-Barnum(ed) Barnum!"

DENVER PUBLIC LIBRARY, WESTERN HISTORY
COLLECTION, NATE SALSBURY COLLECTION, NS-47

To this day, there is still controversy as to whether Buffalo Bill would have wanted to be buried outside of Denver.

As the herds of buffalo became so alarmingly depleted, Buffalo Bill was said to have kept the largest herd of the animals remaining. He used them for his show and bred them to help rebuild their numbers.

During the next several years, Buffalo Bill built a home near Cedar Mountain, Wyoming, and the town eventually took on the name of Cody. He spent time there when he could, and the local population was proud that he made his home there.

For almost thirty years the Wild West Show ran successfully; but Buffalo Bill was aging, and his health gradually weakened. During the last couple of years of the show, his funds were running low, and he and his wife went to stay at his sister's home in Denver. One of Cody's friends was *Denver Post* co-owner Harry Tammen, who had made him a loan to help keep the show going. Unfortunately, the contract for the loan included the rights to the show and to the use of Buffalo Bill's name. As Bill's life wound down, Harry Tammen held a note for $20,000. Cody was distressed over this, and some believe it may have hastened his death.

When Buffalo Bill Cody died at his sister's home at 2932 Lafayette Street in Denver on January 10, 1917, he was seventy-one years old and virtually penniless. Telegrams poured in from friends everywhere, including the king of England, the kaiser of Germany, President Wilson, governors, generals, and senators. His sister, Louisa, upon announcing her brother's death, announced that he would be buried atop Lookout Mountain, west of Denver.

This news came as a shock to many of Cody's friends. What about his birthplace in Iowa? And North Platte, Nebraska? It was his home for many years and the site of his first Wild West Show.

Had it even been given consideration? And what about the town of Cody, Wyoming, which Buffalo Bill had founded? The citizens of Cody recalled that Buffalo Bill himself had stated that he wanted to be buried there. People were outraged. How had this happened?

Perhaps Harry Tammen had had something to do with it. Had he bribed Cody's sister? There was no question that the burial site would greatly benefit the location where it was placed. Besides the sentimental value to those who had known Buffalo Bill, the tourist dollars for such a famous landmark would be a financial boon.

Some light was shed on these questions decades later when a reporter from *Time* magazine wrote an article commemorating Cody's one-hundredth birthday. Stirring up all the hard feelings again, the article stated, "Denver's mayor Robert W. Speer was out to claim him. Buffalo Bill, dead and enshrined, would obviously be a great civic asset. Behind Speer, in the shadows, was Harry Tammen, the moving spirit behind the plot to keep Buffalo Bill in Colorado, near Denver."

Indeed, the Colorado Legislature lost no time in passing a resolution allowing Buffalo Bill's body to lie in state in the Capitol rotunda from 10:00 a.m. to 12:00 p.m., Sunday, January 14, 1917. The City of Denver proclaimed that Mayor Speer and Park Commissioner Milburn would donate the Lookout Mountain site on behalf of Denver.

Meanwhile, there were objections. Cody, Wyoming, maintained that in 1902, Buffalo Bill had written about the Wyoming location to his sister Julia: "I have got a mountain picked out big enough for us all to be buried on." And his will, written a few years

COLONEL W. F. CODY

A western icon and showman, William F. "Buffalo Bill" Cody was one of the world's first internationally celebrated entertainers.

later, stated, "I hereby direct that my body shall be buried in some suitable plot on Cedar Mountain."

But in a recently published video, produced by the Lookout Mountain Museum and Grave, there's an audio recording of Cody's friend, Goldie Griffin. She says that Buffalo Bill stood right on top of Lookout Mountain outside of Denver and said he wished to be buried there.

Which is right? Griffin was recorded in 1972, according to the video. And she has since died, preventing further questioning.

Another factor possibly affecting the choice of the final site was the poor financial state of Cody when he died. Transferring his body to another state would have been costly. The Wyoming and Nebraska towns said they were not contacted at all and might have been able to come up with the funds to move the body and create a suitable burial site. As it turned out, Cody's sister Louisa had paid the burial costs, perhaps giving her the right to decide where her brother's grave should be placed. She maintained that Buffalo Bill had talked about the other site in Wyoming but had changed his mind at the last. No one will ever know if this actually occurred. The complaints from Cody, Wyoming, and North Platte, Nebraska, were ignored.

Buffalo Bill lay in state in the Colorado Capitol rotunda on January 14, 1917. Twenty-five thousand people filed past his open casket. The gravesite was prepared, and the snow was finally cleared from it and the roads on Lookout Mountain. The burial was held on June 3, 1917, nearly six months after the funeral! Estimates say that 20,000 people made their way up to the mountaintop overlooking Denver. In 1921 a building called the Pahaska Teepee, which included a gift shop and restaurant, was built to house Buffalo Bill's artifacts.

Because the hostile feelings over the burial site controversy still ran high, there was concern that threats made to steal Cody's body might have some validity. At one point the National Guard was called in to stand guard with an army tank next to the grave! When Cody's wife died in 1921, she was laid next to him on Lookout Mountain. At that time both graves were then covered with a thick layer of concrete as a security measure.

The town of Cody, Wyoming, commissioned a 12-foot high bronze statue of Buffalo Bill on horseback and put it on display in 1924. The Cody Memorial Museum opened there in 1928. On June 26, 1917, North Platte, Nebraska, hosted a two-day reenactment of the Summit Springs Indian Battle. Two hundred actors were brought in for the re-creation. In October of that year, the town voted to create a lasting memorial to Buffalo Bill by creating Cody Park, including the original site of the first Wild West Show.

So the question continues: Did Buffalo Bill really change his mind about the location of his gravesite prior to his death? Louisa, Cody's sister, repeated in her book, *Memories*, that he'd had a change of heart and wanted to be buried on Lookout Mountain. According to Louisa, he had remarked, "It's pretty up there. You can look down into four states." Were these the words of a dying man, too ill to rebuff his sister? Many folks from Wyoming and Nebraska certainly believe this could have been the case. And yet those at Buffalo Bill's Museum and Gravesite in Colorado are just as sure that he is buried there "by his own request." The truth remains unresolved.

CHAPTER NINE
BABY DOE TABOR

H ang on to the Matchless, Baby . . ." That's what the elderly H. A. W. Tabor is supposed to have said to his young wife, Baby Doe, shortly before he died. These words guided her for the rest of her life, even as she finally perished in the cabin next to the Matchless silver mine. She froze to death.

But did Tabor actually utter those words when he died? And if he did, why did Baby Doe follow them when it only led to misery, poverty, and death? From rags to riches to rags again, the final years of her life were an enigma, an enormous puzzle that may never be solved.

Her death triggered an international avalanche of books and newspaper and magazine articles. Even an opera was later written about her life and performed in New York, casting the world-famous Beverly Sills as Baby Doe.

How is it that a woman from a small mining town in Colorado became so well known? What sparked such interest in her life? Perhaps because she was the real-life embodiment of the classic story about the basic human struggle: reaping tremendous success, then enduring tragic failure. She had become one of the wealthiest women in America, her husband being one of the richest silver

This small shack above the Matchless Mine is where the once-wealthy Baby Doe Tabor froze to death in 1935.

tycoons of all time. Or was it that her success was also tainted by scandal? She had gained her wealth by luring away another woman's husband and marrying him in the most public setting imaginable. And what about her name, Baby Doe? Would her drama have held the same allure if her name had been Jane Smith? That such a beautiful, wealthy, fortunate young woman should fall into destitution was simply unimaginable. She was like the *Titanic* that could not sink, yet she did sink. But she had a choice not to sink—or did she?

How had all this happened? And why, in the end, did she seem to choose ruin?

She was born Elizabeth Bonduel McCourt in Oshkosh, Wisconsin, in 1854. The fourth daughter of Irish immigrants and devout Catholics, she was a born beauty. In her young adulthood one of the young men to notice her was Harvey Doe, the only son in a locally prominent Protestant family. The Doe family looked down on "Papists" (Catholics) and the Irish, and so believed that "Bessie" McCourt was not a good match for their Harvey. Beginning a pattern of disdain for the social mores of the day, on June 27, 1877, Bessie became Mrs. Doe in a simple ceremony held at her home. She was twenty-three, and her new husband, twenty-four.

The city of Oshkosh fell on hard economic times when the lumber industry was hit by a depression. Harvey Doe's father's original wealth had come from a stake in a Colorado mine. As the lumber industry hit a decline, the elder Doe decided to return to Colorado temporarily to find another mining stake to shore up the business at home. This decision conveniently tied in with the wedding of his son. The evening following Harvey and Elizabeth's marriage, the young couple boarded a train, along with Harvey's father, and headed west for Colorado. Since she was high spirited and adventurous, this voyage to the Rockies suited the new bride just fine. She later wrote that the first sighting of the Rocky Mountains from the train made her feel that she was fulfilling her destiny.

The newlyweds honeymooned in Denver while Harvey's father went on to Central City. The couple later took the train from Denver to Black Hawk, and a stagecoach from there to Central City. Elizabeth Doe fell in love with the town and the mountains. She embraced every part of the mining atmosphere, from the raw mountain air to the diverse population of immigrants. And she felt the excitement of promising wealth. As a wedding gift Harvey's father gave the newlyweds a piece of his mining property. He expected Harvey to locate new ore deposits and work the mine, and he would give Harvey a large percentage of the gains. Young Elizabeth was thrilled.

Harvey Doe, however, was not motivated to be a miner. The work was hard, and the mine was not instantly productive. Elizabeth Doe began to realize that her husband did not have the same drive and determination that she did. She soon donned men's trousers and shirts and went to the mine to help him. Although her only goal was to succeed, her actions greatly embarrassed her husband. Their marriage began to break apart even as it began.

Sometime during this period, the name of "Baby" was attached to young Elizabeth. One legend suggests that several miners took notice of her as she stepped along the main street in her vivacious manner, and one said, "There goes a beautiful baby!" The name stuck.

But Baby's marriage didn't. By 1880, after the stillbirth of Harvey and Baby's first child, Baby Doe filed for divorce, citing nonsupport as the reason. The elder Doe bought the mine property that Harvey had deeded to his wife and gave the money to Baby. Thus ended her connection with the Doe family, but she would forever be called Baby Doe.

By this time Baby Doe had heard about another mining boom in Leadville, Colorado. She took the money she'd been given and moved there to begin again. Her disappointing first marriage made her look at a future marital partnership in a completely different way. The right man for her would have to be powerful and ambitious. Her drive and ambition could only be satisfied by someone who was himself as determined as she was.

Horace Tabor, lieutenant governor of Colorado and silver mining king of Leadville, appeared to be such a man. He was so rich and powerful that nobody could live in that town without hearing about him. He had built an empire, funding many beautiful buildings, including the ornate Tabor Opera House. He and his strong but quiet wife, Augusta Tabor, were a notable couple. Many knew that Augusta was the strength behind Horace. Together with their one child, a son named Maxey, they were Leadville's first family.

But beneath the calm surface bubbled trouble. The more money Tabor pulled from his mines, the more arrogant he became. Augusta was concerned about his new opinion of himself. He was never smart about money, but now he was beginning to be extravagant and overbearing. She would caution him about his business dealings and his manner of dealing with his employees. Over time Horace viewed her advice as nagging. Tabor had always listened to Augusta's conservative, intelligent suggestions, but so much wealth was now at his disposal that he no longer felt he needed her. He felt he could do anything in business and it would always turn out well.

The Matchless Mine was at this time bringing in about $1 million a year in silver. There seemed to be no end to the fortune. Horace Tabor had invested in property and other mines, but nothing produced like the Matchless. One of his South American mining investments required that he build a railroad to access it. Tabor was cavalier as he approved this expense. He was unimaginably wealthy, and indeed, money continued to flow to Horace Tabor.

His political power increased right along with his fortune. He was already the lieutenant governor of Colorado, and his sights were set on the governor's seat. Nothing seemed to be beyond his

Once one of the country's richest women, Baby Doe Tabor died penniless near her late husband's famous mine, the Matchless.

grasp, except perhaps a happy marriage. It became common knowledge that he and his wife were having difficulties. However, the prim and proper times of the late nineteenth century did not allow for divorce. He knew his chances for the governorship required a stable home life. Divorce was out of the question, although this did not keep him from having a roving eye and dalliances with other women.

But two people of like minds were about to meet each other, with Baby Doe and Horace Tabor on a sort of collision course. It did not take Baby Doe long to hear about the silver tycoon. It was only a matter of time before she would seek him out.

Horace Tabor sat one evening with his friend, Billy Bush, in the Saddle Rock Café in Leadville. It was a regular habit, following the afternoon performance at the Tabor Opera House. Baby Doe had learned of this pattern and knew she would find him there. She came to the cafe and sat near him at another table, waiting for an opportunity to meet him. It did not take long for Tabor to spot her pretty profile nearby, sitting in her fine clothes. Her beautiful young features attracted his attention.

Horace might have dismissed this encounter as just another flirtation, but Baby Doe was staking her life on it. She discreetly but persistently responded to his glances. Soon a note was passed to her table, asking her to join the two gentlemen. Billy Bush would eventually get up and leave, and the night would pass with Horace and Baby Doe involved in deep conversation. The cafe stayed open all night. By morning Tabor had offered to help Baby Doe with her debts and to rent her a suite in the local Clarendon Hotel.

Baby Doe would become Horace Tabor's mistress, and for the next two years, they would meet regularly and secretly. If they were together in public, Baby Doe would wear a veil over her face. Although Tabor might be seen escorting a woman to dinner, it was unknown who she was. Most kept quiet about Tabor's liaisons with other women. It was assumed this was just another of his many philanderings.

But Horace and Baby Doe were falling in love. She was a good match for Tabor's own ambitions, and she encouraged him and praised his every plan and tactic. She had a good head for his business and was always supportive. Tabor had not had this kind of approving attention and intelligent conversation from a woman for a long time. Baby Doe seemed to comprehend his world and enjoyed talking about it. Most importantly, she agreed with everything he did, unlike Augusta.

By 1882 Augusta finally confronted him about his affair. But he was no longer interested in what she thought. He believed that he had become so wealthy and powerful that his moral indiscretion would be overlooked by voters in the upcoming gubernatorial election. He wanted a divorce.

Finally, in 1883, Augusta Tabor gave up and allowed his divorce to be granted. She had fought it on every level but eventually realized that her husband was never going to return to her. By divorcing Augusta and by planning to marry his mistress, Tabor effectively gave up his hope for the governorship, as well as his ambitions for the US Senate. He was headstrong about marrying Baby Doe but was nevertheless surprised that the political world now ignored him. In an odd little twist, Tabor was indeed given a chance to become the Colorado senator, even if only for thirty days. He was appointed to hold the seat until the elected candidate (who was detained with prior business in Colorado) could come to fill the new office. Tabor was angry and hurt that he had been sidelined in Colorado politics but he accepted the position purely so he could have the title of senator for the rest of his life.

Horace Tabor and Baby Doe were married in Washington, DC, during that brief period of time when he was a senator. They hoped that this public display would not only quell the gossips but dispel any doubts about Baby Doe's reputation. Surely everyone would be impressed by their wealth and her elegance.

Thus began more than a decade of the most lavish kind of living. Horace Tabor traveled to Washington, DC, in a private train, which he rented at the cost of $5,000. Baby Doe later arrived on her own private train (but only after it had stopped in Oshkosh, her old home town, so she could show off her new furs and silks). In just six years Baby Doe had risen to improbable heights. Her family boarded the train and rode with her to Washington, DC.

The wedding, held in the Willard Hotel, dripped with ostentation. The invitations had been trimmed in silver and engraved with silver ink. A $90,000 diamond necklace complemented Baby Doe's $7,500 white satin wedding dress. The reception showcased a centerpiece shaped as a huge wedding bell and made of white roses. The cake had a table of its own to support it.

In addition to various congressmen and senators, Tabor had also personally invited the president of the United States, Chester Arthur, to attend. All these men attended the nuptials on March 1, 1883. Most of their wives, however, stayed at home, refusing to give their stamp of approval to the union. Horace Tabor was thirty years older than Baby Doe and considered a disreputable ogre. Baby Doe was seen as a woman of ill repute, an interloper, a marriage breaker.

However, Baby Doe finally had the husband she'd dreamed of. President Arthur was said to have been dazzled by her beauty, and Baby Doe kept newspaper clippings that recorded his compliments to her. It was reported that the wedding was spectacular, even by Washington standards. But the approval from proper society, which Baby Doe so avidly sought, would never come. Not then. Not ever. As she soon found (and to her great disappointment and puzzlement), wealth might matter in business and politics, but among the women of the day, reputation came first.

Baby Doe, however, had spirit, and she relished being referred to as the Silver Queen. Regardless of the snubs by the jaunty "old guard" in Washington, DC, and Colorado, she had only just begun to make her mark.

First came a new home on Capitol Hill in Denver, the finest, most prestigious location in the city. The Tabor mansion took up the whole block on Thirteenth Street between Grant and Sherman. A three-acre front lawn, fenced by a brownstone wall, held a hundred live peacocks. Said to be the "finest residence in the state," the house was staffed by a dozen servants. Five oil portraits of Baby hung on the walls of the main floor.

The many carriages owned by the Tabors were manned by footmen dressed in scarlet. One favorite carriage was painted black with white trim and the interior was upholstered in white satin. Another was dark blue with gold stripes. Baby Doe chose a carriage according to her choice of apparel for the day.

In 1884 the Tabors' first child, Lillie, was born. Five years later, she had a new little sister, Silver Dollar. Both girls were christened in a $15,000 layette fastened with gold and diamond pins. Jeweled necklaces and diamond baubles were part of their everyday wardrobe.

Baby and Horace spent most of their time at the Tabor Grand Opera House that they had built in Denver. They hobnobbed with the Barrymores and other celebrities who entertained there.

Meanwhile, Horace Tabor's fortune was still growing, in spite of their enormous spending. At its height, his income was about $4 million a year. There was nothing too lavish or expensive for the Tabors to have.

The extravagant displays of wealth overshadowed some of the truly good works Tabor and Baby Doe did. Tabor gave generously to charities and to friends who needed support for their business ventures. He was often not repaid. While some considered this bad business, Tabor realized he had been lucky to come into such wealth and was not afraid to share it.

As the 1880s came to an end, the Colorado silver economy was showing signs of instability. Baby Doe and Horace chose to ignore these omens, however, and had become complacent about their wealth. But politicians were pressing for the country's currency to be backed only by gold. In 1893, after Congress repealed the Silver Purchasing Act of 1890, the value of silver plummeted—as did Horace Tabor's fortune.

Cash flow from the Tabors' property and mining holdings stopped. Bills began going unpaid. Creditors were demanding their due. Like dominoes, one failure precipitated another. Horace had built an empire based on silver. When the bottom fell out, he was ruined. For a time he tried to cover the expenses with loans, but as his holdings became worthless, no more credit was available.

Electricity, water, and gas bills went unpaid. Workmen came to turn off these services for Baby Doe's home. Horace could no longer make deals to cover his debts, and he had no savings put aside. The Tabors were destitute. They moved from their mansion into a small shanty. Horace found work as a laborer, and then, as a favor, a former political acquaintance appointed him the Denver postmaster. For a time, they were able to move into the Windsor Hotel and live an above-average existence. But Horace fell ill and died after just a year and three months in his new position.

It was 1899, and Baby Doe watched as her husband was honored with a funeral and procession that included more than 100,000 mourners. She had to be carried away from his gravesite late in the evening after everyone else had left.

Baby Doe slid into a decline that would last for the next thirty-six years. She moved herself and her daughters back to Leadville, placing her hopes on the old Matchless Mine. She seemed to believe that if she could only get it running again, things would be better. But even her daughters eventually left Leadville (to live with relatives) rather than watch their mother pine away.

Baby Doe rarely left the cabin by the mine. The Matchless represented everything that had made her life grand. She wandered the town of Leadville in rags, too proud to accept charity, apparently oblivious to the fact that her groceries were being paid for by anonymous neighbors.

In the winter of 1935, Baby Doe was found frozen to death in her cabin after a neighbor noticed that there was no smoke coming from the chimney.

Why did Baby Doe die destitute? Did Horace Tabor really tell Baby Doe to "hold onto the Matchless"? Nothing supports this idea. In fact, at the time of his death, he no longer owned the property. Perhaps out of pity, the new owners had simply allowed Baby Doe to live there while it was not in use.

Why didn't Baby Doe remarry? Baby Doe had offers of marriage after the death of Horace Tabor. She was still a marriageable woman at age forty-five and still pretty. Why did she choose not to take advantage of these other opportunities? Maybe she had, indeed, truly loved Horace Tabor. Despite her reputation as a gold digger, perhaps her broken heart would not allow her to marry another. There was an innocence about her as well. If she had been the wily hussy that many believed, wouldn't she have found another wealthy man to provide for her?

Could Baby Doe have been able to begin anew, even without a husband? Bright and astute, she was said to have been offered financial help from friends. She refused these gestures, yet she was likely knowledgeable enough to start some type of business. Or capable of having a job.

But, finally, was she mentally ill? Baby Doe's emotional state would have certainly been in great upheaval. Her losses included her wealth, her home, and her husband. Throughout her life she had exhibited a strong will that might have made her appear to be more resilient than she really was.

Baby Doe Tabor was likely a very misunderstood woman. She was ruled by her passions, anxious for acceptance by her peers, pining away for a husband and a life that could never again be hers. And if Horace Tabor did not tell Baby Doe to hold on to the Matchless, why did she? Perhaps it was because she lost her emotional tether. She may have been unable to hold on to reality any longer. Was it that Baby Doe was so sad that she simply went mad?

Only in death did Baby Doe find the recognition and public fascination that she so desperately sought. She would have been pleased that her life became the center of media coverage, books, and an opera. The legend of Baby Doe remains one of Colorado's greatest romances and, sadly, one of its greatest tragedies. It also is one of its greatest mysteries. No one will ever know for sure why her life ended as it did.

CHAPTER TEN
WHO WAS
ANTOINETTE PERRY?

How does a little girl who was born along a dirt street in the late 1800s, at the base of the Rockies, in Denver, Colorado, end up having the now internationally famous Broadway Tony Award named after her? Many details are missing about this "unknown yet famous" woman, making it a mystery to many how all of this transpired. Yet it did.

When asked, most people think the Tony Award must be named for a man, considering the spelling, and of course the Hollywood Academy Award is called "Oscar," another male name. Still others think the word is meant to suggest the more classy or trendy inference of being fashionable and high-society. But few are able to speculate beyond that. Indeed, Antoinette Perry's nickname was Toni, eventually respelled as Tony, but how would that moniker eventually come to adorn such an ostentatious award?

What the world does know about Antoinette Perry makes this mystery all the more intriguing. It's such an unlikely tale, yet true. Her eventual successes would become legendary.

On June 27, 1888, Antoinette Perry was born in Denver, Colorado, to parents Minnie and William Perry. She was their only child. William was a lawyer and businessman in the newly thriving city. Their home sat along an unpaved street that had first been named Grand Avenue, which reflected the venerable intentions for this location near where the new state capitol building would soon be built just a few blocks away. The street was then renamed Colfax Avenue around 1865, in honor of the soon-to-be-elected US vice president to Ulysses S. Grant in 1868. Colorado would become a state just eight years later, in 1876. Because this was exactly 100 years after the founding of the United States of America, Colorado held the distinction of being called the "Centennial State." By the time Antoinette was a little girl in the early 1890s, she would have been able to view the construction of the many-storied, and domed, capitol building right from her front yard.

Minnie Perry's sister was actress Mildred Hall, who had married George Wessells. George was also an actor, and was said to have performed on the same stage with Edwin Booth, the American Shakespearean actor and brother to Abraham Lincoln's infamous assassin. Mildred and Minnie's father had established the Salt Works Ranch west of Colorado Springs, and they grew up there. Minnie moved to Denver after she married, and Mildred and George continued on running the ranch, while also staying involved in theater.

In the summertime, young Antoinette (by this time often referred to by her nickname of Toni) would leave Denver to visit her aunt and uncle at the ranch. While there, she would accompany them to various acting venues and playhouses throughout the mountains, and also to other parts of the country. It was during these summer visits that Toni fell in love with acting and the theater. She was quoted many years later as saying that she already felt like she was an actress by the time she was six years old.

Toni would return home to Denver at the end of summer, in time for the school year to begin at Miss Wolcott's School. Her persistence in telling her father that she wished to be an actress was not well received, but he decided that a musical career would be more acceptable. So Toni was soon enrolled to study voice and piano at Miss Ely's School in New York City. Later in life, it was said that she had become an accomplished pianist.

And again each summer, she returned to spend time with her parents and her aunt and uncle. When she was at home in Denver, she often gathered her friends to participate in performing plays on her front steps, which she directed. Her parents were chagrinned by these performances along the unpaved street, since it was dusty and Toni's clothes were often soiled. But the shows went on!

Not much more is known about Toni's childhood. It can only be imagined what it was like to live in early Denver, and to see the new city rise up around her. The only form of travel into the mountains each summer was by horse and buggy or wagon. Railroads were being built throughout Colorado and across the country in the late 1800s and early 1900s, so that was another means of transportation. Automobiles were not common until around 1918.

It is presumed that Toni was well trained by her aunt and uncle in all forms of acting and in the study of theater, and she performed in some of her uncle's touring-company plays. She was quite a becoming young woman, with blond hair and clear blue eyes, and her musical training would also have helped develop her stage presence.

When Toni was in her late teens, her aunt and uncle helped her attend her first audition for a play in Chicago. She had immediate success, and was selected to perform for the first time on stage there in June of 1905, in a play called *Mrs. Temple's Telegram*. She was just seventeen years old. That led to her debut performing the same play in New York City a few months later.

Between 1906 and 1909, Toni performed in New York in two additional plays, *The Music Master* and *The Grand Army Man*, and was well received. In the latter, Toni starred opposite David Warfield, a famed actor/director of the era. She was apparently quite observant and always in training, because she would later say how much she had learned from him, and that he made her see what acting was really all about.

But her father hoped for her to lead a more traditional woman's life, and Toni was soon introduced to Frank Wheatcroft Frueauff, president of the Denver Gas and Electric Company. They were married in November 1909 at her parents' home on East Colfax Avenue. Frueauff's wealth propelled Toni from being a well-to-do Denver wife to becoming a wealthy society woman of the world. Her husband became a partner in Henry L. Doherty & Co. in New York City, and an officer and director of more than a hundred other businesses. Toni would soon preside over the running of two homes and a castle! The Frueauff residence was in New York City, and they also frequented their home in Newport, Rhode Island, and acquired a castle in England for occasional visits. Toni became the mother of three daughters, Margaret, Virginia, and Elaine, over the period of thirteen years that she was married. Virginia died in her infancy.

During these busy years as a new wife and mother, Toni did not forget about acting or theater, and was a frequent attendee at the latest new plays in New York. She did make one foray onto the stage in 1920, playing in Brock Pemberton's production of *Miss Lulu Bett*, which later won the Pulitzer Prize. In 1921, Toni attended a concert at Carnegie Hall to see a performance by Sergei Rachmaninoff, the Russian piano virtuoso and composer. Apparently Brock Pemberton was also in attendance and offered Toni his extra ticket. She accepted, and following the concert, she invited Pemberton home to meet her husband. That was the beginning of a lifetime friendship between Brock and Toni.

Unexpectedly, Toni's husband died of a heart attack in 1922. After just over a dozen years as a wife and mother, Toni found her life instantly and forever changed.

Following Frank's death is another period of time when little is known about Toni's life. She was still young at age thirty-four, but what would she do now? It is known that her husband left her a few million dollars from his estate, so she would be able to do whatever she chose. Only one story about this time period, from the summer of 1923, has been related from Toni's grown daughter Margaret (told in the year 2000, when she was eighty-eight years old). She recalled her mother's typically generous ways with her money, when Toni packed up her two daughters, their governess, Brock Pemberton and his wife, and ten others, and took them all on a vacation to Europe for seven weeks.

Upon her return, Toni made a decision that affected the rest of her life: She returned to the theater district and to New York's Broadway for good.

Antoinette Perry

By 1924, she is recorded as having a starring role in the production of *Mr. Pitt*, playing opposite Walter Huston, who later became a famous Hollywood film director. She also starred in Edna Ferber's work, titled *Minick*, and in 1925 acted in three plays: *The Dunce Boy, Engaged*, and *Caught*.

Her friendship with Brock Pemberton expanded into more plays in which Toni acted, and which he produced. Among those were *The Masque of Venice* and *The Ladder*.

The late 1920s were a feverish and competitive time for playhouses and production companies on Broadway. Just prior to the era of talking pictures, an historical all-time high of 264 shows opened in 76 theaters. In 1928 Toni was about to enter a new era in her career, when Brock Pemberton invited her to codirect the play *Goin' Home at the Hudson Theater*. The following year, they had a hit on their hands with *Strictly Dishonorable*, which had a successful run of 557 performances.

Toni had now realized her true calling in directing and gave up acting altogether. By the early 1930s, she was a full-time director. Between 1934 and 1942, she directed several plays, including *Personal Appearance, Ceiling Zero, Kiss the Boys Goodbye, Lady in Waiting*, and *Janie*.

A surprising and largely unknown aspect of Antoinette Perry's life and career during this time period is, even today, mostly undocumented. Most who know anything about Antoinette Perry would think that her acting and directorial achievements by themselves would suggest a good reason for her final honor as the namesake of the Tony Award. But in actuality, this was only a fraction of what Toni gave to Broadway.

With yet more to come in her upward-spiraling directing career, Toni's other contribution took up, by far, the majority of her time and devotion. Her passion was to help young actors achieve their dreams and nurture their talents.

So great was her desire to help that she donated thousands of hours of her time as the chairperson of the American Theatre Council's Committee of the Apprentice Theatre, while also serving as President of the Actors Equity's Experimental Theatre.

Even as early as 1938, Toni was being honored for her untiring support of theater. A gala was held at New York City's Ritz-Carlton Hotel to celebrate her work in helping more than a thousand young actors. She is known to have personally helped many of them financially, from providing hotel rent to offering whatever else they might need to get acting jobs.

Another organization that Toni supported was the American Theatre Wing. Although it had been founded in 1917 to aid in World War I efforts, it came back into full swing prior to World War II. To support the US troops, it held dances and teas and concerts. But its greatest support came from its now famously known Stage Door Canteens. Apparently, Toni was one of the biggest forces behind this idea, which provided military personnel a place for relaxation and entertainment, and was hosted by volunteers from the Broadway theater. Well-known actors such as Al Jolson, Marlene Dietrich, and Dorothy Lamour hobnobbed with the young troops to give them moral support. These canteens were located throughout the country, in New York, Hollywood, Boston, Washington, DC, Philadelphia, Cleveland, Newark, and San Francisco. As their popularity increased, two more canteens were established in Paris and London.

A movie made in 1942, *Stage Door Canteen*, featured famous actors Helen Hayes, Katherine Hepburn, Benny Goodman, and many others. The earnings were used to provide entertainment to the troops in Europe. At the war's end, the American Theatre Wing helped many returning service people with acting classes and other means of support.

But Toni's finest success in the theater world also came about during these same years when she was mentoring new young actors. Enter Mary Coyle Chase: a young playwright also born and raised in Denver, Colorado, who had written a play, a comedy called *Harvey*. It featured a six-foot, one-inch-tall invisible rabbit named Harvey, who was a constant companion of a slightly tipsy man named Elwood P. Dowd. Although Toni had not known Chase in Denver, since Chase was several years younger, the unpolished script got Toni's attention.

Toni had been having great success in directing several plays into the early 1940s, and she saw *Harvey* as her next hit. She was right—in 1944, she directed and coproduced the monumental new play that captivated Broadway audiences, and would have Hollywood hoping for the rights to produce it on the big screen. *Harvey* ran for 1,755 performances, the longest-running hit at that time, and it won the Pulitzer Prize for that year.

Toni had many testaments to her fine qualities as a director, even though women in that position were few. She had a particularly deft hand with comedy. She was said to have been a good communicator and was a natural at teaching timing. She was considered tough, and would even shout and scream to make a point. She snapped at one actress who had held her breath in the wrong spot in the script. She warned her that if she held her breath there, the audience would hold their breath, too. Then she told her to ride out that pause, and ride over the little laughs and go for the big one. Toni had a natural knack for how to get the most from her actors.

But the play *Harvey* and the continued work of the American Theatre Wing would long outlive Antoinette Perry. She died of a heart attack in 1946, a day before her fifty-eighth birthday. Although she had been having health issues for years, her death came unexpectedly. By the time of her death, Toni had directed thirty plays over a span of eighteen years.

A few years earlier, she had changed the spelling of her nickname from Toni to Tony. A nationally advertised hair product had come onto the market named Toni. She was unhappy with the similarity to her own name, so she changed the last letter of hers to a "y."

After Tony's death, the Broadway community was stunned and saddened. It was felt that some kind of honor needed to be bestowed for her legacy to Broadway. The American Theatre Wing decided to create an award for excellence in theater that would bear her name, the Antoinette Perry Award. In 1947, these first awards were paper scrolls, given out along with a token gift, and were presented in front of an audience of 1,200 guests. Brock Pemberton handed out the first award and called it a "Tony."

By 1949, a metal medallion hung from a hook on a small base replaced the scroll; it was engraved on one side with the comedy and tragedy masks (representing theater), and the likeness of Antoinette Perry on the other side. More recently, it was decided by the American Theatre Wing that a place for the recipient's name and winning category was needed, so Perry's profile was removed to provide space. It is still officially called the Antoinette Perry Award, but at the televised ceremony in modern years, her full name is never mentioned. As a result, most viewers of this awards program are completely unaware that Tony was a real woman of amazing theatrical talent from Denver, Colorado.

The Salt Works Ranch is still in existence and remains the longest-operating originally settled ranch in Colorado. In 2005, Antoinette Perry was inducted into the Colorado Women's Hall of Fame.

Although most people will never know the answer to the question, "Who was Antoinette Perry?," you now know more than most.

CHAPTER ELEVEN
BRIDEY MURPHY

On the evening of November 29, 1952, Virginia Tighe sat in a hypnotic trance in a living room in Pueblo, Colorado. The hypnotist had asked her to go back to when she was a small girl, then to her babyhood. Quite experimentally, he had then asked her to go back further in her life, "to some other place, in some other time." Virginia began to speak in a child's voice with an Irish accent. Startled, the hypnotist asked her name and where she lived. The small voice said, "Bridey, I'm Bridey Murphy." She continued, saying that she lived "in Cork. . . . It's in Ireland."

Colorado fell into the national spotlight quite surprisingly in the spring and early summer of 1956 when *Life* magazine ran an article with the headline, "Bridey Murphy Puts Nation in a Hypnotizzy!"

This article and others like it were written following the success of the 1956 bestseller, *The Search for Bridey Murphy*, by hypnotist Morey Bernstein. In it the author revealed that a woman from Pueblo, Colorado, whom he had placed under hypnosis, had shared intimate details of her "past lives" in Ireland. Bernstein's research had proved that her stories, her Irish brogue, and even her archaic vocabulary were all authentic.

The nation was mesmerized by this amazing exposé. Bernstein's book sold more than 170,000 copies. Thirty thousand copies of Virginia's recorded statements under hypnosis had also been sold.

The eyes of America seemed to be riveted on Colorado. While interest in hypnotism had been waning, it was now back on the front pages, put there by what was being called "age-regression" hypnosis. The phenomenon of Bridey Murphy spawned countless imitators, and hypnotists began showing up in living rooms, nightclubs, and theaters across the country. "Come As You Were" themed costume parties became popular. Record albums featured songs about this newly famous woman, including "The Ballad of Bridey Murphy" and "The Love of Bridey Murphy." A new drink was being ordered in bars, the "Reincarnation Cocktail."

But was there any truth behind the sensationalism?

Hypnotist Morey Bernstein was a businessman in Pueblo, Colorado, a partner in the Bernstein Brothers Equipment Company. Virginia Tighe was a wife and mother living in the same small city. She had always lived in the United States and had never traveled to Ireland in her life.

In 1950 Bernstein had witnessed a very convincing hypnotic feat at a dinner party. More out of a desire to prove that hypnotism was a hoax, he began researching the subject. But the more he studied, the more he came to believe it might actually have some validity. On one occasion when his wife was having a migraine headache, he decided to try to rid her of it through hypnosis. While she was in a trance, he had told her the headaches would disappear. Upon awakening, she announced that her headache was gone.

By the time Morey Bernstein's and Virginia Tighe's paths crossed, Morey had helped alleviate many people's health complaints. He had also begun to become interested in age-regression hypnosis.

Morey and his wife decided to invite Virginia Tighe and her husband to their home. Virginia had been hypnotized by Morey before and had shown an ability to go into a deep trance easily. And Morey had done some regression work with her in which he had asked her to recall her childhood. She had been able to remember very detailed events from years before.

But when he asked her to go even further back, prior to her birth, she began to speak in a child's Irish-accented voice. Little "Bridey Murphy" apparently had a mother, father, and brother, and they lived in a white, wooden house in Cork. She went to school at Mrs. Strayne's Day School where she learned "house things" and "proper things." She knew that she was eight years old and that the year was 1806.

As Bernstein continued to question her, he learned that Bridey had grown up to marry Brian MacCarthy, a barrister. They moved to Belfast and, even though she was a Protestant, she had attended St. Theresa's Church with her husband. The priest, "Father John," was a close friend of theirs. She had no children but led a good life. At age sixty-six she had died after falling down a flight of stairs.

Morey Bernstein asked her if she could recall her burial. She said, "Yes," and then described how she had watched them "ditch my body." Afterward, she said she was able to see everyone at home but was unable to speak to them. She also said that she felt no pain and did not need to eat or sleep. She also had known that Father

John had died but was unsure of the date since time meant nothing to her in her afterlife state. But after his death, Father John had come to her, and they had been able to talk as they had when they were alive. She said that she had spent her time waiting until 1923 when she had "become born again" in Iowa, as Virginia Tighe.

In a second session, Bernstein asked Virginia if she could remember a time before she was Bridey Murphy. She said, still with her Irish accent, that she was just a baby, dying. She could not recollect her name or what year it was. She just knew she had died as an infant. And she could not recall anything before that life.

Morey Bernstein questioned "Bridey Murphy" further. She said she ate muffins for breakfast and lived in a neighborhood called the Meadows. St. Theresa's Church was a twenty-minute walk from her home. She recalled the names of villages, rivers, and lakes. She recited a prayer said before meals, recalled a small cup called a "brate" used when making a wish, and said that her favorite dance was the "Morning Jig." Bernstein asked her to remember the jig so she could perform it after she awoke. Later, after Virginia was fully conscious, he asked her to dance. Remembering nothing about the session, she was quite surprised by the suggestion. But she got up and danced a lively jig, ending in a jump and bringing her hand to her mouth. When Bernstein asked why she had done that, she replied that it was a "yawn," but she didn't know why she had done it!

Bernstein held three more tape-recorded sessions with Virginia. When he played the tapes back to her, Virginia felt momentary disbelief and shock when she heard herself speaking in an Irish child's voice. But she ultimately accepted the possibility that she may actually have lived other lives.

In these final sessions Bernstein's focus was to ask for details that could be verified. He wanted to check out Bridey's information and see if it matched real sources from that time. For example, Bridey had said one of her favorite books was *Sorrows of Deirdre*. Bernstein was able to confirm that during Bridey's life (1798–1864), this book had indeed been quite popular. He found the same with an Irish folk legend she had mentioned, as well as a reference to the *Belfast News Letter*. Bernstein referenced maps for the names of towns and rivers that Bridey had mentioned. Indeed, they were where she had said they were.

Still other pieces of information were verified. Unfamiliar words she had used turned out to be appropriate in Ireland at the time. "Chirurgen" meant surgeon, and she referred to a man as a "tup," meaning "chap." Both words had been the archaic form of the presently used words. The cup she had mentioned as a "brate" was actually called a "quate"—close enough to be considered correct since she was remembering it as a child. And her earlier use of the phrase, "ditched my body," was a reference to mass burials in ditches during the Irish famine. It would have been a word that someone of Bridey's time might have said. "Barrister" was used for lawyer and "linen" for handkerchief.

Believable as this story seemed to be, there were many detractors. Once the book was published, reporters wanted to talk directly to Virginia Tighe. But Bernstein had agreed not to call her by her real name and, in the book, had referred to her as Ruth Simmons. When the press couldn't find a Ruth Simmons in Pueblo, further searching led them right to Virginia Tighe. Virginia fended off the interviewers, even turning down offers of large monetary payments.

In Denver a reporter named William (Bill) Barker was sent to Ireland by the *Denver Post* to search for evidence that would either prove or discredit the Bridey Murphy story.

When he returned, he wrote a long article about his findings. He said that all of her information had been substantiated. Even the most obscure names, places, and shops had checked out. He had scoured the old records to find forgotten information that was no longer included on modern maps or documents. There was no question in Barker's mind that Virginia's story was true.

But still there were skeptics. Religious groups against the idea of reincarnation denounced Virginia, and certain newspapers were disputing her as well. Virginia had spent her childhood in Chicago, before moving to Colorado. The *Chicago American* found information in the city records that it felt might explain various parts of her story. It said a woman named Bridie Corkell had lived across the street from Virginia Tighe when she was growing up. Corkell's maiden name had apparently been Murphy. And Virginia was found to have had an Irish aunt who might have told her stories from her homeland. As a girl Virginia had taken elocution and dance lessons. Maybe she had learned an Irish jig or even to speak in certain dialects. Many began to believe that Virginia's memories of a past life were really just recollections of her life as a child.

Morey Bernstein and *Denver Post* reporter Bill Barker were upset over this slanderous approach to the facts. The tabloids had not actually proved anything but had just printed many disconnected pieces of information that had been enough to cause doubt and confusion. The *Denver Post* decided to stick by its story, sending a reporter named Bob Byers to Chicago, where Virginia had grown up, to investigate these allegations.

He found that Virginia's aunt Marie was of Scottish-Irish descent, but had been born in New York and had never been in Ireland. And although Bridie Corkell indeed had a maiden name of Murphy, little Virginia wouldn't have known this since she had been just a small child when her family had lived near this grown woman. Murphy is also one of the most common names in Ireland. Virginia's childhood elocution lessons were for speaking proper English, not dialects, and her dancing lessons (in which she was enrolled as a teenager) were for the Charleston and the Black Bottom.

But while the *Chicago American* had not really disproved Virginia's experience, the public nevertheless concluded that the whole thing had been either a hoax or a trick of childhood memory. By the time the *Denver Post* published its follow-up story, headlined, "Chicago Newspaper Charges Unproven," America had largely dismissed the whole thing.

After all, Virginia Tighe herself had stated that it was all very hard to believe: "The thing that makes all this so difficult is that I'm not ready to say whether I do or do not believe in reincarnation. My husband and I have tried to keep open minds. We only wish they'd let us keep the record straight as well."

Since 1956 other well-documented occurrences have been reported suggesting that past-life experience could be factually based, but it is still considered random and unlikely. Was there really a little girl in Cork, Ireland, named Bridey Murphy who was reborn and became Virginia Tighe in Colorado? No one will ever know for sure.

CHAPTER TWELVE
THE UFO AND
SNIPPY THE HORSE

On October 12, 1967, the *Denver Post* published the results of an opinion poll regarding an incident it had been reporting in its newspapers. A three-year-old Appaloosa mare named Snippy, which had lived on Harry King's ranch 20 miles northeast of Alamosa, Colorado, had been found dead under mysterious circumstances. One-third of the respondents believed the incident to be a hoax, another one-third found it unexplainable, and the final one-third believed it had occurred as the result of a flying saucer.

Vibrant, young, and full of energy, Snippy had been beloved by her owners, Nellie and Berle Lewis. Harry King was Nellie's brother, and Nellie and Berle would ride Snippy whenever they visited the ranch from Alamosa. Snippy had spent her days running free in a ranch pasture, trotting up to the ranch house in the evening to drink from the trough. On the evening of September 7, 1967, however, she hadn't come up for a drink. Nor did she appear the next evening. On the following morning, Harry King decided to drive out and search for Snippy.

He found her lying dead in the shadow of Mount Blanca. When he inspected the carcass, King was horrified and sickened by what he saw. He knew he needed to tell someone about this right away. He called Nellie and Berle. Then he related his sad discovery to his eighty-seven-year-old mother, Agnes, who also lived on the ranch. Agnes recalled that on the first night when Snippy had not come in from the pasture, she had seen a large object flying over the ranch. She hadn't had her glasses on so she couldn't say for sure what it had been, but she'd been struck by the fact that it had made no sound. She had thought no more about it until that moment.

Nellie and Berle came to the ranch and accompanied King to where Snippy lay. The horse's body lay on its side, appearing normal, except for one thing. The head and neck had been stripped of flesh. From the shoulders up, there was no hide, hair, nor flesh. The exposed bones had been scraped clean and were bright white. Even the incision at the neckline was so exact that it might have been done with a scalpel.

To add to this already incomprehensible sight, there was no blood on the ground and no tracks around the carcass. Nellie and Berle were astonished.

Closer inspection of the ground revealed circles pressed into the ground. They were about 2 inches across and 4 inches deep. They were arranged as parts of larger circles that were about 3 feet around. Across an area of about a half-mile, fifteen of these circles were burnt into the ground. Berle said that they "looked like they'd been made by exhaust pipes."

A nearby bush had been flattened, and the sandy ground seemed to have been smoothed out. Then Nellie found a piece of horse flesh. It was sticky, and a light green paste came off on her hand. She said it made her hand red and burned her skin. When she dropped the flesh and rinsed her hand with water, the burning stopped.

Later Nellie found some kind of implement that had horse-hair on it. When she picked it up, it also burned her hand.

Then they came upon Snippy's tracks in the dirt. The filly had obviously been running. But then the tracks stopped abruptly about 100 feet from the spot where her body had been found.

Over the next several days, the exposed bones turned pink. The puzzle was deepening. Everyone at the King Ranch wanted help in determining just what had happened to one of their favorite horses.

First, they had called the sheriff, Ben Phillips. He had dealt with odd occurrences before. Ranches out in this open country were subject to all kinds of attacks on their animals. Bears, mountain lions, and coyotes were common predators. When Phillips heard some of the specifics of this case, he felt sure it must have been lightning that got Snippy. It happened to stock animals frequently.

But Nellie Lewis was not willing to accept that. She hoped to find someone who would come out and look at Snippy before they rushed to a conclusion. Duane Martin, a US Forest Service ranger, came to the ranch about two weeks after the tragedy. He admitted he was baffled. He had seen what lightning does when it kills animals, and he agreed that this looked totally different from anything he'd ever seen. Martin happened to have a Geiger counter with him. After seeing all the evidence before him, he decided to check for radiation in the area. The readings he took over the horse's carcass were negative, but his counter began to register radiation near the circles with the burn marks. The same was true around the flattened bush.

The newspapers finally got wind of the story and visited the scene. The *Pueblo Chieftain* headlined an article, "Dead Horse Riddle Sparks UFO Buffs." And the Associated Press ran the story nationally. The media were the first to actually mention the UFO theory.

How else could all these odd events be explained? Interestingly, this was not the only event to spark UFO speculations. Near the end of September, two Denverites using a telescope claimed to have seen a glowing and brilliantly colored disc floating east of the mountains. They said they saw it two nights in a row. And within a few days of that sighting, in early October, a superior court judge, Charles E. Bennet, and his wife and his mother all saw three reddish orange rings cross the Denver night sky. The judge reported the rings were flying in a triangular formation and moving very fast and making a humming sound. In Alamosa, far south of Denver, some residents believed they had seen a UFO explode in the sky.

By October 8 the *Denver Post* had reported the story about Snippy and the incident in Alamosa. The newspaper suggested that forensic scientist Dr. Edward Condon at the University of Colorado in Boulder look into the events further. Perhaps he might be able to either explain or discredit the story, said the *Post*.

Condon did not respond, but other investigators did. The National Investigations Committee on Aerial Phenomena (NICAP) sent a four-man team to the King Ranch. The investigators interviewed Harry King and Nellie and Berle Lewis, and they took photos, soil samples, and other evidence. A Denver pathologist offered to do an autopsy, if he could remain anonymous. (Perhaps the doctor thought his name might be tarnished if his colleagues found out he was involved.) He supposedly found that there were no abdominal organs in the horse and no fluid in the spinal column. These odd findings were never substantiated.

Finally, Dr. Robert O. Adams, a veterinarian from Colorado State University, agreed to do an autopsy. He determined that Snippy had been suffering from a severe infection in her right flank. He deduced that Snippy must have fallen down from the pain of the infection and then been euthanized by a passerby. Adams theorized that animals then picked the bones clean on the upper portion of the carcass.

But why was no blood ever found? And why were there no human or animal tracks? King and the Lewises could not accept the findings of the veterinarian. They also felt they would have known if Snippy had an infection.

The public wasn't satisfied either. Snippy's demise was still a mystery, and the explanation seemed to be left to anyone who cared to venture a guess. A columnist at the *Denver Post* decided to give it a try. Based on the reports he had read, Robert W. "Red" Fenwick said that the whole thing was a prank. He thought Snippy had been shot with a tranquilizer, hoisted on a block and tackle, and dipped head first into a vat of acid. This, he said, would dissolve the flesh and drain the fluids. Acid would account for the remnants of flesh, tool, and scorched holes. Easily obtainable ground uranium could be sprinkled on the ground to create the radioactivity and to lend added mystery. This hoax theory did have some credibility, but most thought it did not fit all the evidence.

During all this excitement and speculation, Alamosa was experiencing a huge increase in tourism. There were some who believed that the business community had dreamed up the whole episode, at the expense of Snippy's life.

UFO sightings continued to occur through the fall. Conejos Canyon, south of Alamosa, was especially active. Unexplainable, multicolored lights were seen. And a number of silent flying objects continued to be spotted near where Snippy had died.

One group, the Aerial Phenomena Research Organization (APRO), thought the most important aspect of the case was that no footprints or tracks had been found around the horse. This certainly supported the idea of some paranormal possibility, they said.

Since 1967 many other horse and cattle mutilations have been reported from remote ranches. Often these reports have stated that the animals were cut with surgical precision, and that their sex organs, lips, tongues, and eyes were removed, and their carcasses drained of blood. In these cases, too, no tracks or footprints have been found. Sometimes circular indentations have been reported around the area.

Most ranchers who own the land where these events have occurred and who have lost animals have never been satisfied with the official explanations. Whatever happened, it remains a mystery. Only Snippy knows what she saw before she died that night.

CHAPTER THIRTEEN
THE IDLEDALE SAMOVAR AND THE MISSING PROFESSOR

S ometimes one mystery leads to another. In this case, a Russian samovar, originally made for Czar Nicholas II, sat quietly in a little antique shop in Idledale, Colorado, in 1968. This bit of information alone is rather astounding, even without further elaboration.

A samovar is an ornate brass hot-water urn. It was used in Russia and parts of China to heat the water for tea among the social elite. It was usually placed at the center of bulging buffet tables or on doily-bedecked parlor tables. Because it was a centerpiece, the samovar was commonly designed by artists, with embellishments and engravings etched on its top and sides.

How would such an artifact, the property of a Russian czar of the nineteenth century, end up halfway around the world in the twentieth century? And how did it come to rest in a tiny little town in Bear Creek Canyon near Denver?

Idledale, Colorado, sits on a pretty mountainside above Bear Creek. Originally a resort town in the 1930s and 1940s, it began attracting permanent residents in the 1950s and 1960s. Of its 400 or so residents, many commuted daily into Denver (about 15 miles away) for employment. The town boasted a post office, a two-room school, two small grocery stores with gas pumps, and two antiques shops. One of them, Hanes House Antiques, sat alongside Bear Creek Canyon Road, which continued on to Evergreen. Tourists traveled the scenic route and often stopped to browse through the shop.

On April 25, 1968, Evergreen's *Canyon Courier* newspaper ran a feature story written by Joan (Pierron) Murphy, headlined, "Mystery, Intrigue, and Two Russian Samovars!" The editor of the newspaper had apparently heard that there were two samovars in the nearby mountain area and had asked the freelance feature writer to delve into it.

One samovar was said to have been originally owned by Leo Tolstoy, the famous Russian author, and it could be found at the Cradle, a shop located in South Turkey Creek (another canyon west of Denver). The second was the one originally owned by Czar Nicholas II, on display at Hanes House in Idledale. These shops were within several miles of each other, and unbeknownst to each shop owner, both had samovars that had belonged to famous Russians!

The origins of the Tolstoy samovar were easily traced. The owner of the Cradle, Miro Salva, was the nephew of Dr. Dushan Makovitzky, Leo Tolstoy's personal physician. He had acquired the samovar from Tolstoy and later given it to the Salva family. This samovar was not for sale.

But the second samovar at Hanes House in Idledale was of mysterious origins. The owner of the shop, Marguerite Hanes, had bought it from an army colonel who had brought it back from

Europe at the end of World War II. He had claimed that it was the true samovar of Nicholas II, czar of Russia.

It appeared authentic. A double-headed eagle, the official seal of the czar, glimmered on the front. Below it, printed in the Russian alphabet, were various inscriptions. There were also seals from nine different expositions where the samovar had been displayed, also in the Russian language. Two were from Russian fairs in 1893, and the others were from expositions that took place from 1895 through 1904. One was from the Nashville, Tennessee, Centennial Exposition of 1897; two were from French expositions; and the last was from London, at the International Food Exposition at the Crystal Palace.

To have the samovar authenticated, Mrs. Hanes found a noted expert, Thomas Riha, a professor of Russian and art history at the University of Colorado. Professor Riha helped establish the authenticity of the Hanes House samovar, as well as appraise its value. Mrs. Hanes placed it for sale at $500. It was later sold to a prominent family in Denver.

But how had the samovar of Czar Nicholas II come into the hands of an army colonel? During the war, many artifacts changed hands, and the actual details about the acquisition of the samovar were never recounted.

But even as this original mystery of the samovar's authenticity came to be solved with the help of the University of Colorado professor, another mystery was about to occur. This time it involved the professor himself.

In March 1969, just a year after the incident regarding the samovar, Professor Thomas Riha was reported missing. Stories were printed in the *Denver Post* and *Rocky Mountain News* for

Thomas Riha, a University of Colorado professor, disappeared in 1969 under mysterious circumstances.

several days running. All were full of intrigue as the details of the case became available. On March 15, forty-year-old Thomas Riha was last seen about a half hour after midnight when he had left the Boulder home of friends with whom he'd had dinner. Riha did not show up to his classes the next day. When his home was investigated, the lights had been left on as though he may have left in a hurry. He was never seen again.

The more searching that occurred, the odder the whole mystery became. Within just a few weeks, Thomas Riha's house and car were sold by "an acquaintance." And his beloved art collection was donated to the Denver Art Museum! Some friends maintained that Riha traveled to his home country of Czechoslovakia regularly. He often had said that he'd been contacted by Czech, US, and Soviet intelligence agents, each hoping to enlist him in obtaining and carrying information. He apparently laughed about this. It had become a joke among Riha and his friends.

It was also learned that Riha had been married just four months earlier and was already in the midst of getting a divorce. His wife, Hana, had left for New York after a recent incident where she had been seen one night crawling out of a window of their home and screaming. A neighbor (also a CU professor) and his wife had helped Hana get out of the window and had taken her into their home.

The Boulder Police had been called but had come to no specific conclusions other than that she and Thomas Riha were soon to be divorced. It was dismissed as a domestic dispute.

When the president of the University of Colorado, Joseph Smiley, was contacted to comment on the disappearance of Riha, he calmly replied that he had been informed there was nothing to worry about, that Riha was "alive and well." When pressed as to his source, Smiley would only say that it was a government official.

Also adding to the mystery, a woman name Gayla Tannenbaum was apparently at the house that evening when Mrs. Riha had crawled out the window. After Thomas Riha disappeared, she turned up again at the home, supposedly picking up his mail. When asked about his whereabouts, she said that he was in Montreal, Canada, and was doing fine.

Meanwhile, the University of Colorado Art History Department was left in the dark. They were angry that, if indeed Riha was doing well, he had left without reporting to them.

Although some reports suggested that Thomas Riha was alive and well, none of his friends in Boulder or at the university were hearing from him, and they were concerned that nothing was being done to find him. Nothing seemed to be adding up. But since there was no evidence of foul play, the Boulder Police were not pursuing the case diligently.

Meanwhile, ambitious reporters kept turning up new twists to the story.

Thomas Riha had received his PhD in art history from Harvard and was hired by the University of Chicago in 1960. He had traveled to what were then called "iron curtain" countries (under Soviet communist rule) including Czechoslovakia where he was born. His mother had lived there until moving to Germany. In 1967 he had accepted a position in the art history department at the University of Colorado. Riha was interested in the art of Russia and other Eastern European countries, and collected important pieces for his own enjoyment.

Friends and associates said that Riha was content in his job at CU. Professionally, he enjoyed his students and was responsible in his duties. His personal romantic life, however, was in turmoil. Not counting his wife, at least four other women in previous relationships had left him. Nevertheless, friends from both the University of Chicago and the University of Colorado were not convinced that Thomas Riha had just walked away from his life without telling anyone.

The CU art history department finally did file a missing-person report on Riha, and the Boulder Police came and took reports from various associates; but one strange occurrence nixed further progress on the case. Gayla Tannenbaum, so often mentioned as a secondary character in this drama, now called the Boulder Police to say that she had received a phone call from Riha, saying he had "gone to the East Coast" and that she was in contact with him. This was enough for the police to halt their investigation.

And yet friends kept divulging new pieces of information that led authorities to wonder whether or not Riha was somehow involved with espionage. A few weeks before his disappearance, for instance, he had claimed that he was "being followed." And another friend, who saw Riha the last night before he went missing, said Riha had lightly referred to the fact that "at best, the life of an agent is ten years."

Riha's nephew, Zdenek Cerveny, who was then living nearby in Lyons, Colorado, felt that something was very wrong. In March 1970 he filed a request to have a conservator appointed for his uncle's estate. Since there had been no will, this would allow his family to deal with Riha's assets. It also allowed a legal way to probe the sale of Riha's house and car and the disposal of his art collection, all of which Cerveny suspected were fraudulently acquired and transferred.

About this same time Riha's mother died in Germany. Before her death she had said that she had never heard from her son after his disappearance. Until then he had always stayed in touch with her regularly.

Interestingly, Gayla Tannenbaum was now awaiting trial for forging three of Thomas Riha's checks and possibly other documents. She was also charged with forgery in documents pertaining to the will of a distant relative. She pleaded innocent by reason of insanity. And indeed, after examination by a psychiatrist, she was deemed less than fit to stand trial. She was committed to the state hospital in Pueblo, Colorado.

Finally, an article appeared in *Time* magazine in early 1970, which again stirred up concerns about Thomas Riha's mysterious disappearance. As a result, phone calls with all types of leads began pouring into the Boulder and Denver police departments. And given that Gayla Tannenbaum's forgery cases were being tried under Denver jurisdiction, the Denver district attorney, James D. "Mike" McKevitt, also became involved.

One of McKevitt's first acts was to follow up on CU president Joseph Smiley's comment that he'd been reassured that Thomas Riha was "alive and well." Looking to verify the information, McKevitt contacted both the CIA and FBI and was now absolutely certain that Smiley had not received information from either

COLORADO MYTHS & LEGENDS

source. (However, it would not be until 1976 that the CIA would admit that it had indeed told Smiley that Riha was "alive and well." It turns out that McKevitt had apparently been told this in 1970 but had been sworn to secrecy!)

And in a final bizarre disclosure, the CIA said the original information about Riha's apparent safety had come from the FBI who had believed the same source that everyone "accepted" at the time: Gayla Tannenbaum. There was no way now to verify her information about why she believed Riha was in Montreal. Following her institutionalization at the state hospital, she had committed suicide in March of 1971.

In October 1977 an army intelligence document was released, having been overlooked by the US Senate Intelligence Committee that reviewed the Riha case. Colorado senator Gary Hart, a member of the committee, had requested the inquiry. Concern had been raised on account of possible threats to national security. The report said that Riha was sighted in a Montreal bookstore in September 1969, and that an army intelligence agent was "pretty sure" that Riha was dealing with the KGB or with groups connected to it.

Senator Hart acknowledged that the inquiry "obviously hasn't solved the Thomas Riha mystery." Myriad questions remain. What was Gayla Tannenbaum's relationship to Riha? Was Riha really spotted in Montreal? Did agents look for him there based solely on Tannenbaum's report? Does the FBI or the CIA know more about what really happened to Riha than has been revealed? Did his mother lie about not seeing him following his disappearance? Is Thomas Riha now living in Russia?

In September 1978, after a filing by Riha's nephew, the Denver Probate Court finally declared Thomas Riha legally dead. Although the possible sightings of Riha were reviewed by the court, they were found to be impossible to substantiate. Meanwhile, Riha had been missing for almost ten years. Cerveny and his sister were found to be his rightful heirs and they received his small estate.

In 1982 a new story appeared in the *Rocky Mountain News*. A memoir written by Gayla Tannenbaum in 1971 had been discovered in the files of her lawyer. In this document, Tannenbaum states that Riha returned to her home in Denver after he had gone to Montreal. He told her that he planned to go to Russia where he had been offered some opportunities, and that his personal life had fallen apart and that his work was no longer fulfilling. Gayla wrote that she was angry that he was going to leave her. This woman (who was, after all, declared insane) said that she had little recollection of what happened next. She remembered driving to St. Mary's Glacier with Riha where they walked and talked, but then she thinks she killed him. Although she described it in great detail, no evidence was found to substantiate it.

Thomas Riha, professor and art connoisseur, had solved the Idledale samovar mystery but would leave no clues to solve his own disappearance.

CHAPTER FOURTEEN
A TRILOGY OF SHORT MYSTERIES

In the nooks and crannies of Colorado, from the bustling downtown of Denver to the remote backcountry, there remain several small mysteries that will likely forever go unsolved—widely divergent in nature.

There's Denver's Colfax Avenue, for instance. Often called the "longest main street in America," Colfax Avenue spans 26 miles, from Aurora on the east to Golden on the west.

But after nearly 150 years of tying the city of Denver together, a mystery still remains about this famous road. In the 1850s, Colfax was called the Golden Road (you ended up in Golden if you went far enough west out of Denver), and then it was later called Grand Avenue. But around 1865 it was renamed Colfax Avenue, apparently in honor of US Speaker of the House Schuyler Colfax, who was touring the West at the time.

Colfax went on to become, in 1868, one of our country's more obscure vice presidents, lasting one term under Ulysses S. Grant. Possibly the most significant thing about him, at least for Coloradans, is the fact that he became the namesake of Denver's historic Colfax Avenue.

COLFAX, HON. SCHUYLER OF IND. LIBRARY OF CONGRESS, LC-DIG-CWPBH-04750

Schuyler Colfax, former speaker of the House of Representatives and vice president under Ulysses S. Grant, was the namesake of one of Denver's most prominent streets.

But why? Why did Denver name one of its most essential streets after a visiting speaker of the House? Colfax wasn't from Colorado, and his connection to the state was almost nonexistent. He was from Indiana and had been elected to the US Congress in 1854, becoming speaker in 1863. But he did have a stepsister who was married to a prominent Denver real estate investor. Because of this connection, Colfax visited Colorado again, in 1868 and 1873. But was this enough for his name to be immortalized by the Denver city council? It seems unlikely.

In 1900 the Denver Tramway and Denver City Railway Company built a trolley system on Colfax. The avenue was paved in 1916, and buses began offering service in 1928. Interstate 70 was built in the 1960s, diverting traffic around Denver rather than through it. Due to lack of attention, Colfax then began to decline, gradually becoming one of the least desirable neighborhoods in the city.

By the 1990s, however, Lakewood, Denver, and Aurora had joined together to help rehabilitate Colfax Avenue. Lakewood encouraged a retro look in new building, while Aurora refurbished large sections of the street, adding tree-lined dividers down the middle. In 2005 Denver adopted new zoning measures that encouraged more pedestrian-friendly development. And in 2006 the famous Tattered Cover Bookstore opened a branch on East Colfax across from East High School.

Schuyler Colfax would certainly be proud of having his name attached to such a living monument. But, again, why was Colfax Avenue named after him in the first place?

Schuyler Colfax had an interest in the West and may have been a politician whom the Colorado Territory courted for favors. It may have wanted to boost its position in vying for statehood. Perhaps Denver officials thought that renaming the street would help the state's cause. Colorado first applied for statehood in 1865, the same year that Colfax Avenue was renamed and the same year as Colfax's western tour. (Interestingly, Colfax County in New Mexico was also named for him, as was the city of Colfax, California, also at the time of this tour.) But if help with achieving statehood was the reason for the street's name change, it didn't help much. Colorado did not become a state for another eleven years.

Colfax Avenue, however, goes on. And regardless of the reason for its naming, it thrives. The many famous people who have lived along this street and the places that have been part of its culture have eclipsed whatever its origins were.

Schuyler Colfax died in a Minneapolis railway station in 1875. He carried to his grave the answer to any political benefit he may have lent to Colorado's future.

Meanwhile, East High School, which borders East Colfax Avenue, matriculated numerous well-known people. The famous actor Douglas Fairbanks Jr. attended East High School. And in the 1960s, so did Judy Collins, the singer-songwriter. Hattie McDaniel, the first black woman to receive an Academy Award (for her role in

It's hard to imagine downtown Denver without Colfax Avenue, often called "one of the longest Main streets in America."

DENVER PUBLIC LIBRARY, WESTERN HISTORY COLLECTION, X-22579

Gone with the Wind) was also an East High alum. And so was 2005 Academy Award nominee Don Cheadle.

Colfax Avenue was also the location for the filming of the movie *Any Which Way but Loose*, starring Clint Eastwood. And the episodes of the revived popular TV series *Perry Mason* were written as TV movies for actor Raymond Burr, who produced and filmed them on Denver streets, including Colfax Avenue.

Entertainers seem to have a special relationship with Colfax Avenue. One little girl named Antoinette Perry was born at 2815 East Colfax Avenue in 1888. She grew up there, studied acting and the theater there, married there, and had her first child there. But upon her husband's premature death, she left for New York where, at the age of thirty-five, she began her acting career on Broadway, soon directing and producing plays. Her contribution to Broadway dramas over the next twenty years endeared her to the theater world. When she died at the age of fifty-eight, she was so missed that the American Theatre Wing created an annual theater award specifically to honor her. They named it the Antoinette Perry Award and dubbed it after her nickname: "The Tony," for outstanding work in Broadway theater.

Golda Meir, a prime minister of Israel, grew up in Denver. So did Madeleine Albright, the first female US secretary of state. And Condoleezza Rice attended Denver University before becoming the second female US secretary of state.

Each of them would have driven along Colfax Avenue in their drives around town. It's nearly impossible not to!

Colfax Avenue represents more than a century and a half of vibrant living for people of every age, race, gender, and future. Hail to Colfax Avenue. May its legend continue to grow and may the mystery of why it got its name forever keep historians guessing!

◆━━◆

In the southwest corner of Colorado is another site of intrigue that has endured even beyond the recorded history of Colorado. It harbors mysterious ruins of a different and once thriving culture.

Hovenweep, a Ute word for "deserted valley," lies just northwest of Mesa Verde and was part of the same Anasazi (or ancient Puebloan) cultural system. The Hovenweep inhabitants, similarly, abandoned their settlements about ad 1300, never to return.

Hovenweep differs from Mesa Verde because it does not have plentiful deep canyons and cliff dwellings. Instead, it has shallow

Abandoned around AD 1300, the Hovenweep ruins are one of Colorado's most enduring mysteries.

canyons and a more open landscape. And unlike other Anasazi locations, the ruins that remain today include hundreds of one-, two-, and three-story towers spread out over the landscape. They stand individually, rising like castle turrets into the sky.

Why did the Anasazi build hundreds of towers in Hovenweep? And why were some built as circular, round silo shapes, others in a D shape, and still others in squares?

Building homes of native rock had become the common practice on the mesa tops throughout Mesa Verde and the other Anasazi sites in the Four Corners region of Colorado, Utah, New Mexico, and Arizona. But why did the "tower design" evolve only at Hovenweep during the last 100 years before the Anasazi finally left the area forever?

Tree ring dating indicates that the Hovenweep towers were built between ad 1163 and 1277, and that the majority were constructed after 1230. Further archaeological research provides evidence that the Anasazi of this area had begun to move from the mesa tops to communities located around towers at the heads of canyons.

A persistent theory surrounding this move to the canyon heads—and the move into the cliffs at Mesa Verde—is derived from the same evidence. Drought. Lack of rain and severe drought conditions had gradually increased during the last years of Anasazi habitation of these regions. Relocating to the canyon heads in Hovenweep was a short-term solution to this expanding problem. Water from underground springs was collected in dams and reservoirs at the canyon heads next to the towers. Today, tower ruins still stand along the banks of springs, as well as on the mesa tops.

Archaeological speculation has suggested several possible uses for these towers. Defense, food storage, communication, ceremonies, and astrological calculation have all been considered. Since the towers have almost no windows or doors (some without any openings at all), they seem to have been meant for some type of special use that required an impenetrable enclosure.

Although none of these possibilities can be substantiated, proximity to other known buildings provides the basis for some theories. For example, a few of the towers have been found to have underground tunnels connecting them to kivas. While this suggests that the towers might have had a ceremonial use, most of the towers are not located or joined to other kivas.

Yet all of the towers have been found to contain some remnants of cultivated crops. The towers that were built later were not only better constructed but appeared to have had a variety of uses. Some archaeologists believe these were used for grinding rooms, tool-making centers, and possibly storage areas.

Defense remains a strong possibility for the creation of the towers since they sit within known village sites and next to springs and water storage areas. Evidence points to violent activity of some sort. Possible conflicts with outside tribes, or even other Anasazi interlopers, would have made the towers useful for observation and protection. Could the varied square, round, and D-shaped design of the towers had something to do with better visibility? No one knows.

Some towers have portholes that could have been used to mark summer and winter solstices and spring and fall equinoxes. When sunlight penetrated these openings in some of the towers, accurate calendrical information could have been forecast for crop planting and harvesting. And lunar portholes that would have accurately plotted the movement of the moon have also been found.

But none of these theories fully explains why these towers were built or why they were built in such profusion only in the Hovenweep area. For now the imagination is the best time machine to take us back and explore why the Anasazi built these edifices. The Hovenweep towers will likely hold their secret forever.

The final tale here to be pondered occurred near the town of Granby, Colorado, on the Western Slope. It is a legend that persists and continues to keep us intrigued.

In a pasture northeast of Granby in 1920, a rancher named Bud Chalmers was removing rocks from an excavation he planned to use as a reservoir. He'd been pitching stones onto a pile all day when he heaved one that was far heavier for its size than all the rest. He decided to take another look at it.

Its weight definitely distinguished it from the other rocks of Colorado granite, and as he washed it off, he noticed its dark color. But he soon realized that he was holding some type of artifact that had carvings all over it!

Measuring about 1 foot high and 1½ feet wide, a smiling primitive face was staring back at him from the stone. Cut into each side were little ears and three-fingered hands. On its front were unintelligible symbols, and carved on the back were two figures—a prehistoric hairy mammoth and a long-necked dinosaur.

The stone became quite a novelty, sitting on Bud Chalmers's front porch for the next few years for all the local residents to view. By 1926 it wasn't given much attention anymore. But when a new resident named Henry F. McKnight bought a nearby ranch, he visited Chalmers and saw the stone. He offered $300 for it, and Chalmers accepted.

Then in 1969 a story appeared in *Old West* magazine, entitled "Runestones and Tombstones," in which the story of the "Granby Idol" was retold. It so happened that the author of the story was Lela Smith MacQuary. She had seen the stone nearly fifty years earlier when it was sitting on Bud Chalmers's porch and had found it interesting enough to take a few photographs of it.

A couple of interested readers contacted Mrs. MacQuary and received permission to show the photographs to experts. Dr. Cyclone Covey, author of a book titled *Ancient Chinese Sojourns in America*, verified that the symbols on the stone were ancient Chinese writings from 1,000 years earlier. His belief was that the "Granby Idol" was an artifact from ancient Chinese trans-Pacific voyages. His book had theorized about this possibility. Other proponents of this theory believed that the Chinese and Japanese often sailed to the Americas as early as the fifth century ad. Thor Heyerdahl of Kon-Tiki fame had similarly believed in these early voyages.

Was the "Granby Idol" proof of these voyages? How could this stone with ancient writing have ended up in Colorado? Dr. Covey believed that the skill of ancient Chinese mariners made these voyages probable, but no artifacts had been found to prove it. He felt that the photos of this stone lent credibility to his speculation. His final conclusions were that the stone was some type of a marker for travelers and that the stone was made of fine-grained dolomite, a heavy stone common to northern China. Words on the stone that he was able to translate were "north," "river," "fruit," and "fish." He believed that such stones might have been placed at periodic locations to guide travelers who ventured inland.

Unfortunately, the "Granby Idol" itself was never again found, and Dr. Covey could not prove his speculations. The potential for further excavation in the region where the relic was uncovered was also lost. In 1946 a dam was constructed to create Granby Lake, which now covers the site.

Only the photographs, if still believable in this modern day of photographic technology and tampering, suggest that this "carved rock" ever existed. Henry F. McKnight, the buyer of the stone, had said he wanted to place it in a museum "back East." So far, it has not turned up. But perhaps it is sitting in storage in some unknown location or even masquerading as a "gnome" in someone's backyard garden.

One thing is for sure: The "Granby Idol" may be smiling because it still has a secret to tell.

BIBLIOGRAPHY

THE GREAT SAND DUNES

Hafnor, John. *Strange but True, Colorado*. Fort Collins, CO.: Lone Pine Productions, 2005.

Jessen, Kenneth. *Colorado's Strangest: A Legacy of Bizarre Events and Eccentric People*. Loveland, CO.: J.V. Publications, 2005.

THE ANASAZI

Ayer, Eleanor. *The Anasazi*. New York: Walker, 1993.

Crewe, Sabrina, and Dale Anderson. *The Anasazi Culture at Mesa Verde*. Milwaukee, WI.: Gareth Stevens, 2003.

Larson, Timothy. *Anasazi*. Austin, TX.: Steadwell Books, 2001.

Noble, David Grant. *Ancient Colorado: An Archeological Perspective*. Denver: Colorado Council of Professional Archeologists, 2000.

THE REYNOLDS TREASURE

Collier, William Ross, and Edwin Victor Westrate. *Dave Cook of the Rockies*. New York: Rufus Rockwell Wilson, 1936.

Drago, Harry Sinclair. *Lost Bonanzas*. New York: Bramhall House, 1966.

Everett, George G., and Dr. Wendell F. Hutchinson. *Under the Angel of Shavano*. Denver: Golden Bell Press, 1963.

Jessen, Kenneth. *Colorado Gunsmoke*. Boulder, CO: Pruett Publishing Company, 1986.

THE LOST JOURNEYS OF UTE CHIEF COLOROW

The Golden Transcript, 1864.

Pettit, Jan. *Utes: The Mountain People*. Boulder, CO: Johnson Printing Company, 1996.

Simmons, Beth, PhD. *Colorow! A Colorado Photographic Chronicle*. Morrison, CO: Joint Publication of the Jefferson County Historical Commission and the Friends of Dinosaur Ridge, 2015.

P. T. BARNUM

Autobee, Robert. *If You Stick with Barnum: A History of a Denver Neighborhood*. Denver: Colorado Historical Society, 1993.

Uchill, Ida Libert. *Howdy, Sucker: What P. T. Barnum Did in Colorado*. Denver: I. L. Uchill, 2001.

LOUIS DUPUY AND THE HOTEL DE PARIS

Riddle, Ellen Ray. *Louis Dupuy and His Souvenir of France*. Mission Viejo, CA: John Ray Riddle, 1985.

The State Historical Society. *A Fragment of Old France*. Boulder, CO: Johnson Publishing Company, 1954.

THE MOTHER CABRINI SHRINE

Keyes, Frances Parkinson. *Mother Cabrini: Missionary to the World*. San Francisco: Ignatius Press, 1959.

Miceli, Mother Ignatius. *Cabrinian Colorado Missions*. Boulder, CO: D & K Printing,1996.

———. *Colorado and Mother Frances Xavier Cabrini*. Boulder, CO: O'Hara, Inc., 1980.

Missionary Sisters of the Sacred Heart of Jesus. *Novena Prayers and Sketch of the Life of Mother Cabrini*. Chicago: Mother Cabrini League pamphlet.

BUFFALO BILL'S GRAVESITE

"By His Own Request." (Video recording.) *Buffalo Bill and Lookout Mountain*. Denver: Media Dynamics, 2000.

Carter, Robert A. *Buffalo Bill Cody: The Man Behind the Legend*. New York: J. Wiley, 2000.

Shields, Charles J. *Buffalo Bill Cody*. Philadelphia: Chelsea House Publishers, 2002.

Sorg, Eric. *Buffalo Bill Myth and Reality*. Santa Fe, NM: Ancient City Press, 1998.

Baby Doe Tabor

Bancroft, Caroline. *Silver Queen: The Fabulous Story of Baby Doe Tabor*. Boulder, CO: Johnson Publishing Company, 1980.

Burke, John. *The Legend of Baby Doe*. Lincoln and London: University of Nebraska Press, 1974.

Hall, Gordon Langley. *The Two Lives of Baby Doe*. Philadelphia: Macrae Smith Company, 1962.

Who Was Antoinette Perry?

Gustaitis, Joseph. "Antoinette Perry: The Woman Behind the Tony." *American History Magazine*, April 1997.

Nassour, Ellis. "Antoinette Perry Makes a Name, the Tony Awards Memorialize Tony." *TheaterMania*, May 2000.

Bridey Murphy

Barker, William J. "The Truth about Bridey Murphy." *Denver Post* supplement, March 11, 1956.

Bernstein, Morey. *The Search for Bridey Murphy*. Garden City, NY: Doubleday, 1956.

Brean, Herbert. "Found: Bridey Murphy." *Life* magazine, March 19, 1956.

Kutz, Jack. *Mysteries and Miracles of Colorado*. Corrales, NM: Rhombus Publishing Company, 1993.

The UFO and Snippy the Horse

Kutz, Jack. *Mysteries and Miracles of Colorado*. Corrales, NM: Rhombus Publishing Company, 1993.

The Idledale Samovar and the Missing Professor

Cunningham, Allen. "Riha Friends Launch Desperation Hunt." *Rocky Mountain News*, January 30, 1970.

———. "Riha's Neighbors Looked On in Disbelief." *Rocky Mountain News*, February 22, 1970.

Freed, David. "Was Thomas Riha Slain by Lover?" *Rocky Mountain News*, July 11, 1982.

Gillies, Fred. "CIA Admits Its 1969 Riha Role." *Denver Post*, November 9, 1976.

———. "Riha's Ex-Wife Fears Missing Professor Dead." *Denver Post*, January 25, 1970.

Lindsay, Sue. "Thomas Riha Declared Legally Dead." *Rocky Mountain News*, September 13, 1978.

Murphy, Joan. "Mystery, Intrigue, and Two Russian Samovars!" *Canyon Courier*, April 25, 1968.

A Trilogy of Short Mysteries

"Colfax Avenue—Mainstreet Colorado." (Video recording.) Denver: Havey Productions, 2000.

Davies, Nigel. *Voyagers to the New World*. Albuquerque: University of New Mexico, 1970.

Goodstein, Phil. www.colfaxavenue.com/history.php.

Kutz, Jack. *Mysteries and Miracles of Colorado*. Corrales, NM: Rhombus Publishing Company, 1993.

McGinty, Bernice and Jack. *True West* magazine, 1971.

Noble, David Grant (ed.). *Mesa Verde and Hovenweep*. Santa Fe, NM: Ancient City Press, 1985

Trimble, Stephen. *The Bright Edge: A Guide to the National Parks of the Colorado Plateau*. Flagstaff: The Museum of Northern Arizona Press, 1979.

INDEX

ABOUT THE AUTHOR

Jan Elizabeth Murphy is the author of *Outlaw Tales of Colorado: True Stories of the Centennial State's Most Infamous Crooks, Culprits, and Cutthroats,* also by TwoDot. She was born in St. Louis, Missouri, to parents with the wanderlust, and had already gone on three Colorado vacations with them by the time she was eight years old. On these trips, she went to the top of Pikes Peak, built dams in the creek next to the family's cabin in Evergreen, and camped for two weeks in Rocky Mountain National Park.

Jan was thrilled when her family moved to Bear Creek Canyon in the Colorado mountains near Denver. She attended one of Colorado's last two-room schools, which had a real iron stove in the kitchen used to cook lunches. A few years later she rode the school bus down the canyon road every day to attend Red Rocks Jr. High School. The view from her classroom window was of the famed Red Rocks Park and Amphitheatre.

She attended Bear Creek High School and went on to college at the University of Colorado in Boulder. Her career took her to Washington, DC, New York, and Boston, but she eventually returned to Colorado where she renewed her enjoyment of hiking. This included a five-day camping and hiking trip along a fifty-five-mile segment of the Colorado Trail, led by Gudy Gaskill, the founder of the trail.

Jan has traveled throughout the United States, and to France, Luxembourg, and Mexico, but her favorite place is still Colorado. She taught Colorado history and hiking classes in local community education programs, and at Lockheed Martin Astronautics Evening Institute for six years. Jan served on the board of directors for the Jefferson County Historical Society for seven years.